DID ROMANS DESIGN THE SPACE SHUTTLE?

THE ROMAN EMPIRE

FASCINATING FACTS AND
EVERYDAY PHRASES EXPLAINED

Peter Ryding

PATHFINDER

Published by Pathfinder Partners Ltd.

ISBN 0-9551525-5-0
ISBN 978-0-9551525-5-9

Designed by Oxford Designers & Illustrators

Cover design by Baseline Arts Ltd., Oxford

Illustrated by Ray and Corinne Burrows

Printed and bound in Germany by GGP Media GmbH, Pößneck

For
Richard the Roman historian

Acknowledgements

I would like to take this opportunity to thank everyone who has so enthusiastically embraced and supported the WINKT project from its inception: the many dinner guests who have patiently listened, challenged and in some cases politely fallen asleep whilst I have shared my latest linguistic discoveries; Steve, the guy in the pub who challenged me to write the first book; Peter at ODI, who has been a stalwart supporter and always kept a sense of humour despite everything (and there have been lots of 'things'!); Corinne and Ray, my artists; Gillian, who has challenged and checked and added her own ideas despite an apparently endless set of iterations.

Of the many others, who are too many to fit on one page but who have encouraged me throughout, I would like to thank Crisspy the Duck and his friends, Simon, Neil, Spence, Tim (Nadia), Sam (Jo), Hutch, Gordon, Alexander The Great and Henry V, all of whom have played their roles, plus the designer of the keel of the boat, without whom we would all have drowned.

Also thanks to the many members of WINKT the club who continue to write in with both intriguing questions and fascinating discoveries.

Thanks to every one of you.

Contents

Preface

Imagine you are a foreigner who has just learnt the basics of the English language. You proudly walk into a room of native English speakers and listen to their conversation.

'Was it a cock-up you ask? I should bally say so! But it's a good job he had an extra string to his bow because they had him running from pillar to post in that job. His boss's ideas were so off the wall that it wound him up something proper. No wonder he's legged it!'

You may well think you had been on the wrong course!

But it's not just the phrases we use that make English tough to learn and a joy to use. Our language has absorbed more subtleties and richness from other nations than any other. Indeed, English is by far the most widely used official language in the world. We also have the largest vocabulary in the world, at over 250,000 words in the *Oxford English Dictionary*. Having said that, we each tend to pick from our own favourite 2–3,000 most of the time, rarely stepping outside our comfort zone. To put this into context, Shakespeare used over 21,000 words and a top scrabble player will know over 80,000 words!

So, with all this richness and precision at our fingertips, such that we can intuitively distinguish between a simple 'room' and a grander 'chamber' (in a way that many languages cannot), what do we do? We dredge up obscure phrases that often arose for reasons that are no longer relevant and that people don't really understand anyway. Or, even worse, ones that they misunderstand. For example, imagine the foreigner who overhears that something is 'cheap at half the price'. What does that mean? Is it saying that it would be cheap if it was half the current price? In other words, that it is expensive? Or is it saying that it is cheap because it is half the price you were expecting to pay? If *we* are not sure – what chance do foreigners have?

In many cases phrases have simply gone wrong over the ages. For example, take 'the exception that proves the rule'. Pardon? Are we saying that finding an exception to a rule somehow proves that the rule is correct? Surely that has to be utter tosh!

It is only through patient research and an understanding of our heritage that we can make sense of such expressions. In this case the explanation goes back to the Normans' invasion of England in 1066 and their desire to have a clear set of rules with which they could govern the country. The trouble was that the barely literate Anglo-Saxons had few written laws. Most were simply 'known' to those who dispensed justice. However, the Normans passed a law that said that if someone could prove beyond doubt that there was an exception to a law, then by implication that would prove, in another case, that the law did exist. For example, a trader who had a pass allowing him to travel at night after the curfew hour – literally, the hour at which the fire (*feu*) had to be covered (*couvert*) – would prove that the law of curfew did exist. This in turn would enable the

prosecution of someone who broke the curfew. Hence, an exception to a rule does not in fact prove that the rule is correct. However, it does prove that the rule exists!

Yet another example of things going wrong is the phrase 'Don't spoil the ship for a hap'orth of tar!' Now, tar may be cheap, but a hap'orth (that's half a penny's worth for those born after 1980) of it does not go far when you are trying to waterproof an entire ship! In fact, by digging into the past we discover that the saying originally referred not to a ship at all but rather to a humble *sheep*! The reason is that just about the only help you could give a sheep with an open sore or wound was to slap on a dollop of tar. This would at

least close the wound and was of course worth doing – especially given the financial value of sheep in medieval days, when they produced the vast majority of England's income. After all, without them we could not have afforded to fight the French through the Hundred Years War! And let's face it, you don't often get the chance to humiliate the entire French nation like we did at the battles of Crécy, Poitiers and Agincourt! Well worth a hap'orth of tar so that we don't spoil the *sheep*!

However, the story is not all mistakes and misunderstandings. Some derivations are a sheer joy to discover. Like the Greek god who used to jump out on humans and scare them away

from his personal harem of nymphs and dryads. His name was Pan, from which we get the word PANIC! Or the need for sailors to be flogged up on the main deck because down below in the cramped conditions there was NOT ENOUGH ROOM TO SWING A CAT – o' nine tails! Why nine tails? Because the Royal Navy decided that the normal three-headed scourge representing the Father, the Son and the Holy Ghost was not 'holy enough' for wicked sailors and so created a 'trinity of holy trinities'. Hence nine tails that left deep scratches on the skin just like the claws of a CAT. And of course the scars would then stay with the troublemaker for the rest of his life, making him a MARKED MAN!

There is also the wonderful realization that so often when different words sound similar they are in fact the same word,

or at least come from the same original source. For example, cheque books, checkmate in chess, checklists, rain checks, the checks (bills) you get in American restaurants, the game of chequers, checkered patterns, the Chancellor of the Exchequer, Chequers pub signs, the prime minister's country house Chequers and simply 'checking something out', all derive from medieval military coups in Persia! Wonderful!

Having studied our language hand in hand with our history for over two decades, I am still surprised, amazed and delighted at what treasures I uncover on a regular basis. Creating this series of books has been a massive and painstaking undertaking, bringing a lot of pleasure and at times a lot of frustration. I just hope that you have fun with the books and that you will find something fascinating, insightful and intriguing within each book that makes you say 'Well, I Never Knew That!' And of course, when you do, please tell your friends and join WINKT the club at www.winkt.com – and vote for WINKT to become a new word in the English language! Thank you for doing so.

Don't just enjoy the English language – CREATE IT!

How to use this book

This book has been written in a unique format so that you can enjoy it in several different ways:

1. You can **read it cover to cover** as an adventure into the rich stories and interconnectedness behind our language.

2. You can **flick to a page** and discover fascinating facts bit by bit.

3. You can **study the pictures** at the start of each chapter and try to work out the sayings that await you inside.

4. You can **seek out specific words** and sayings via the index.

5. You can **use it as a quiz book** on your own or spoken out loud with friends, by reading each paragraph and then stopping just before the CAPITALS reveal the answers.

6. You can just leave it in the loo for everyone to enjoy. But beware – your guests may not come out for some time! And, of course, when they do they are bound to say – **'Well, I Never Knew That!'**

1

Early Rome

The historical beginnings of Rome
are hard to disentangle from legend,
but some of their earliest practices
and ideas have stayed with us
ever since.

Well, I never knew that . . .

. . . Rome's kings went too far – beyond the pale

Around 1200 BC a beautiful Greek princess called Helen was kidnapped by a Trojan prince and taken to his father's city of Troy. In response the Greeks created an armada of over 1,000 ships full of soldiers to win her back. Hence the phrase 'THE FACE THAT LAUNCHED A THOUSAND SHIPS'.

After ten years of siege the Greeks tricked the Trojans into taking a giant wooden statue of a horse into their city not realizing that it was full of Greek soldiers – who came out at night and defeated the Trojans. From this we get the term used for a computer virus that secretly enters your computer and then attacks it from inside some time later: TROJAN HORSE; also the phrase that warns you to be wary of unusual gifts from seeming well-wishers: BEWARE OF GREEKS BEARING GIFTS.

One of the victorious Greek heroes was called Aeneas. He took his share of the treasure from Troy to Italy, where he founded a nation called Alba Longa. Four hundred years later two of his descendants argued over who should rule. One had a daughter called Rhea Silvia and it was agreed that if she had a son that child would become king. However, she was tricked into becoming a priestess at the temple of Vesta. These priestesses looked after the eternal flame of the city but were also sworn to celibacy. Hence the term VESTAL VIRGINS. The punishment for breaking this oath was a painful death. However, the god Mars Sylvanus came to Rhea Silvia one night and nine months later she secretly had twin boys called

Romulus and Remus. Clearly she could not keep them, and so they were abandoned to die in the wilderness. However, they were found by a female wolf who suckled them and raised them into young men. The two brothers decided to create a city but argued over which of two hills to build it upon. Romulus killed his brother and then went on to found a city named after himself that was to have a long and illustrious future: ROME. To this day the symbol of Rome is a SHE-WOLF SUCKLING TWO BABIES. Again according to legend, Rome was founded on 21 April 753 BC – and so Rome is one of the few cities in the world with a BIRTHDAY.

Romulus attracted many soldiers to his city but very few women and so he tricked a nearby tribe called the Sabines to attend a lavish celebration. He attacked the men, took 800 of the women and then forced them to have children with his soldiers. This has inspired many paintings and sculptures called 'THE RAPE OF THE SABINE WOMEN'.

Pales was an important Italian goddess when Romulus founded Rome. He named the main hill of Rome – one of seven – after her: the PALATINE HILL. Subsequently, the emperor Caesar Augustus built his massive personal and official residence on the hill, and this vast building became known as the Palatium. Via a translation into French and then into English, this gives us our words PALATIAL and PALACE.

The word *pales* was also used to describe long poles and stakes. Hence the Roman throwing spear was called a PILA (and, incidentally, the male member is called a PHALLUS). Roman military forts would usually have a row of defensive stakes around the camp, tied together to form a defensive wall. Such walls were called PALISADES. Interestingly, when

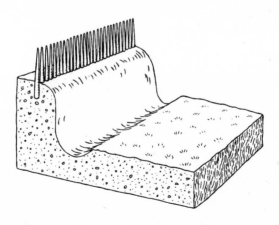

William the Conqueror first came to Britain he did not have time to build stone castles and so built wooden castles instead, using such stakes for protection. In Ireland he placed a ring of stakes around the city that is now Dublin and warned both his people and the barbarians who lived beyond it that he claimed the land within the stakes and would kill any savages who entered it. Equally, he could not guarantee the protection of his own people if they went beyond the line of stakes. Hence the phrase meaning outside a safe area: BEYOND THE PALE.

The first rulers of Rome were kings, but after 250 years of increasingly tyrannical rule an especially unpopular King called 'Tarquin the Proud' was expelled in 509 BC. The supreme authority was then split between two people who ruled together, so that no one person would ever again wield total power over the city. These two were supported by a council of 300 elders from the best families in Rome. Using the word for an old man, *senis* (from which we get the word senior), this council of elders was called the SENATE and its individual members were called SENATORS. These senators

held their positions for life, but in contrast the two leaders were elected annually – another way of ensuring that no one person could ever again dominate the Roman people. These two leaders were also expected – indeed, constitutionally required – to consult and gain the support of the Senate in governing, and so they were called CONSULS. The fundamental principle of this form of government was to give the power back (*re-*) to the *public* and hence it was called the Roman REPUBLIC.

Another of the seven hills of Rome had a great temple built upon it. Because this temple was so important, this hill was then seen as the chief of the seven, and so, using the element *cap-* meaning head (as in the word for chopping off someone's head: DECAPITATE), it was named the CAPITOLINE HILL. More than 2,000 years later, Thomas Jefferson and his colleagues emulated much of the Roman system of government in formulating the new United States Constitution, including a senior house of senators called the SENATE. Eventually a building was designed to house the US Congress in Washington DC; it was modelled upon Roman architecture

and used the same name given to the Roman temple: THE CAPITOL. The name Capitol is also used in several other US states for the building that houses the state government. Cities throughout the world that host the 'head' (*cap*) of government are also called CAPITAL CITIES. This is why Washington is the capital of the USA even though New York is the larger and better-known of the two cities.

By the 3rd century BC the major commercial power in the Mediterranean was Phoenicia, a trading nation based on the coast of Turkey. Its people were called Phoenicians, or by the Romans in a derogatory sense as Phoeni or Poeni. The city grew rapidly through commerce, and eventually an exiled Phoenician queen set up another city in modern-day Tunisia, called CARTHAGE. Its inhabitants became known as Carthaginians, and rivalry with Rome was intense. There were three vicious wars between Carthage and Rome which the Romans called, after the original name of the people, Poenic Wars – known to us as the PUNIC WARS.

Well, I never knew that . . .
. . . Hannibal's elephants didn't go under the yoke

The first Punic War started in Sicily in 264 BC and ended 20 years later with little achieved by either side. In 218 BC a dispute over ownership of gold mines in Spain led to the second Punic War. This time a Carthaginian general completely surprised the Romans by marching his entire army, including elephants, into northern Italy via the Alps. His name was HANNIBAL. This wrong-footed the Romans and resulted in a war in Italy that lasted for over ten years.

Incidentally, the traditional depiction of these elephants with mini-'castles' on their backs is wrong. When Alexander the Great defeated the Indian emperor Porus, he integrated into his army the kind of war elephants the Indians had used: a large breed that carried castle-shaped 'turrets' on their back, as depicted in many Indian chess sets. However, Hannibal's elephants were of a smaller breed from North Africa that is now extinct; these were not strong enough to take the weight of a 'castle', just a driver and one or two fighting men sitting astride it like a horse.

Anyway, following several defeats a new Roman general, called Quintus Fabius Maximus, worked out that if his army could avoid any major battle with Hannibal, over time the Carthaginian soldiers would become homesick, tired and demotivated, while the Roman troops could constantly be reinforced and refreshed from their nearby home city. Fabius then instigated a series of small battles to chip away gradually at Hannibal's army, knowing that he could not get reinforcements from Carthage in Africa. The ploy worked, and this strategy of trying to wear an opponent down while avoiding any single decisive confrontation has given us the phrase FABIAN TACTICS. Incidentally, George Washington used a similar successful strategy in the War of American Independence, deferring direct battles against the British while his army was too weak to win. He became known as the 'American Fabius'. However, the Roman Senate soon became impatient and wanted a decisive victory, so they replaced Fabius with a hot-headed general and a larger army. Almost straight away Hannibal defeated the Romans in a great victory beside the lake of Cannae. This victory, against all odds, altered the course of the war and thereafter Hannibal terrorized the Italian peninsula for many more years. Since that time, a phrase has been used to describe a critical event against the odds that has proved to be the turning point of someone's military or political career: THEIR CANNAE. It was such a skilful and over-whelming victory that it is still taught to all British army officers and it was not until the bloodiest battles of World War I that so many soldiers were killed in one day again!

Now, the Romans had a military tradition whereby defeated enemies had to pass under a spear held up by two more spears stuck in the ground. The top spear was purposely positioned low to ensure the enemy had to bend down awkwardly to get through. So when Hannibal beat the much larger Roman army at the Battle of Cannae, all the Roman prisoners were forced to crouch under a low archway made of weapons and farming yokes to humiliate them and reinforce the fact that they had been totally defeated. This is where we get the expression UNDER THE YOKE. This was such a

humiliation for the Romans that when the soldiers returned to Rome the whole legion was punished in several different ways. One of these was that for the next 10 years the soldiers were forbidden to sit down while they ate their food!

After this defeat the Romans re-adopted the Fabian tactics, and after years of ineffective campaigning Hannibal was forced to retreat to Carthage, just as Fabius had predicted.

Eventually the Romans took the war to Carthage in North Africa, defeated the army and destroyed the city. The general Publius Cornelius Scipio then gave an instruction that has come through the ages as an expression of total devastation: 'LEAVE NO STONES STANDING', literally meaning that every building was demolished down to just one layer of stones with no stone left standing on another. The Romans also ploughed salt and rubble into the fields to ensure that the city of Carthage would never again re-emerge. This was seen as such a successful mission that the general was awarded the title by which he is better known to history: SCIPIO AFRICANUS.

Incidentally, from the Latin word *rodere,* meaning 'to gnaw', we get the word for a gnawing animal: RODENT. The closely related word *radere,* meaning to scrape, gives us the word for the total destruction of a city and the 'scraping' of it off a map: RAZE, as in to RAZE A CITY TO THE GROUND. From the same root we also get words for a blade that 'scrapes' off bristles, RAZOR, and an item that scrapes off pencil marks, ERASER.

While the African city of Carthage never recovered, the Carthaginians did start again on the Spanish coast, where they built a city called New Carthage. However, this was soon followed by the third and final Punic War, which ended in total victory for Rome and the complete end of the Carthaginian people.

The Roman Republic subsequently worked in various forms and with varying degrees of success until the arrival on the scene of one man. He was nearly assassinated as a child, captured by pirates as a teenager, and eventually changed the Roman constitutional system. He dominated the ancient world and his life has had many repercussions through the centuries ever since. To accommodate this person the two existing consuls, called Pompey and Crassus, agreed to a unique sharing of power among not two people but three. Using the Latin words for three, *tri*, and man, *vir*, this was called a TRIUMVIRATE. Little did they know what the consequences of this would be for them personally, for Rome, and indeed for the world. The person in question was in fact so influential and had such impact that many national rulers have been named after him. These include, in Russia, the CZAR; in Persia, the SHAH; and in Germany, the KAISER. His name was JULIUS CAESAR. **WINKT!**

2

Julius Caesar

If there's one Roman we've all heard of, whether because of the river he crossed, the woman he fell in love with, or the man who killed him – or just because of Shakespeare – it's the first Caesar!

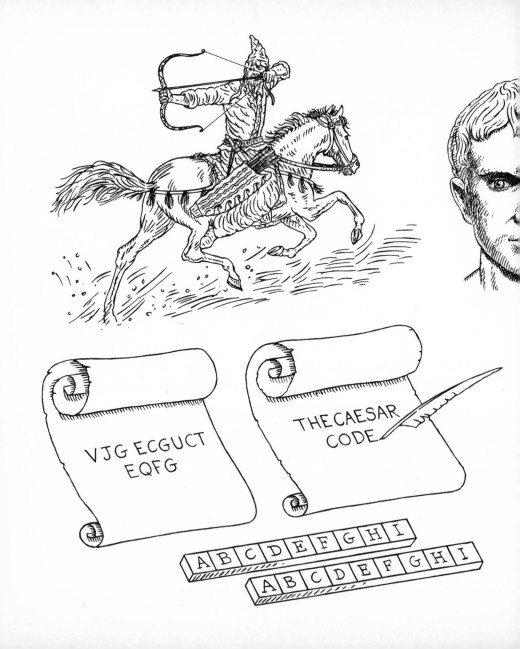

Well, I never knew that . . .
. . . Caesar named the French after a farmyard bird

The consuls Pompey and Crassus were very rich, tough and successful military commanders. Between them they had defeated the famous slave revolt led by SPARTACUS and then crucified 6,000 of the slaves on the main road into ROME. They both had complex financial and political reasons to share power with Julius Caesar, who was an up-and-coming political and military leader, and so they agreed a geographical split of power. Pompey took responsibility for the western territories, including Spain; Crassus took the eastern lands; and Caesar took responsibility for the partially conquered Gaul (modern-day France).

Crassus soon went off to Parthia (near modern Iran) to defeat the local king. But unfortunately Parthia was essentially a desert. Crassus had an army of heavily armoured Roman infantry and the Parthian forces were primarily lightly armoured archers mounted on horseback. These cavalrymen would ride up close, firing arrows, and then, when the infantry tried to charge them, would turn and ride away – still firing arrows as they galloped off. Needless to say the Romans were slaughtered, including Crassus, who died in the desert. From this calamity for Rome a phrase has developed meaning a deadly attack from a distance as your enemy withdraws – often seen in the politics of the Roman Senate: 'PARTHIAN SHOT'. Nowadays it is sometimes bastardized into A PARTING SHOT, A PASSING SHOT, or A SHOT IN PASSING.

Caesar left Pompey in charge of Rome while he attacked Gaul, a campaign he launched in order to win the loyalty of the army and to build up public support and raise his own profile. The area directly north of the Italian peninsula was the first area into which Rome expanded, and when it was subdued was initially called the Province. Later, as the empire expanded, it was called Province One. This area of France is still called PROVENCE.

When the Romans invaded what today is France they found several tribes who used the symbol of a cockerel to inspire their warriors in battle. This appeared on banners and as metal figures on the top of long poles. As a result the Romans referred to these tribes collectively using the Latin word for cockerel,  *gallo,* from which we get the terms GAUL and GALLIC and ultimately GAELIC. In fact the symbol of France is still a COCKEREL.

When Rome conquered south-west France all the way to the Atlantic coast they named it after the Latin for water, *aqua*: AQUITAINE.

When they later came across the western coast of Spain they recognized that this sea was the same ocean that lay to the west of the 'Pillars of Hercules' (what we call the Straits of Gibraltar). This ocean was traditionally named after the lost kingdom of Atlantis; hence we call it the ATLANTIC OCEAN. Knowing nothing of America, they assumed that this was literally the *end of the earth*, and so they named the most westerly tongue of land that extends into the Atlantic Ocean near modern-day Santiago de Compostela just that – *finis terra* or, as we know it, FINISTERRE. Incidentally, the French also have their own Finisterre and eventally the confusion led to the BBC weather forecast for shipping having to stop using this term and start using another instead. They chose the name of a British weather expert: FITZROY. Of course, the British equivalent of Finisterre is in Cornwall: LAND'S END.

Having defeated many of the Gallic tribes, Caesar returned to Italy and was told by Pompey and the Senate (which was largely in cahoots with Pompey) to leave his army outside the borders of Rome and come in, on his own, to discuss next steps. Caesar clearly smelt a trap and decided to ignore the state's instruction and instead marched on Rome with his full army. The critical point occurred when he reached a river that defined the borders of Rome and that he knew he was not allowed to cross with his army. An ancient law, designed to prevent any general threatening a military takeover of Rome, clearly stated that no general could come within a certain distance of Rome with his army without permission. Coming from the north, the boundary for this restriction was the River Rubicon.

Needless to say, Caesar crossed the river and took control of Rome. This action has gone down in history as a crucial part of Rome's history, and an expression has arisen meaning to pass a point of no return: CROSSING THE RUBICON – from the River Rubicon. Incidentally, as he did so, Caesar made a statement to his generals that is still used today, meaning

that an irrevocable action has been made and to some extent the outcome is in now the hands of fate: THE DIE IS CAST.

Pompey realized he was going to lose and so fled Rome, initially to Greece. Caesar pursued him and eventually beat his army under the command of Pharnaces, a friend and supporter of Pompey. Caesar famously reported this campaign with the simple claim *Veni, vidi, vici*: 'I CAME, I SAW, I CONQUERED.' Pompey then fled to Egypt, falsely thinking the Pharaoh would protect him. But instead he was murdered. On arriving in Egypt, Caesar was presented with Pompey's severed head. He also met and instantly fell in love with an ethnically Greek princess of Egypt who was descended from the Greek general Ptolemy, who had been the right-hand man of Alexander the Great. Her name was CLEOPATRA.

Caesar eventually returned to Rome where he became increasingly powerful. However, this also made him enemies, and before long he pushed Rome too far. He used an old provision that had been designed so that in a national emergency the consuls could be given complete executive power by the Senate for a period of up to six months. During this time, instead of *consulting* with the Senate they would *tell* (Latin *dicere*) the Senate what they were doing. This provision was therefore called DICTATORSHIP and the consuls would be renamed DICTATORS. Anyway, Caesar simply decided to take this power for himself for ten years, and the Senate was too weak to say no. However, the move did not go down well and schemes started to develop to murder him.

In the end Caesar was assassinated by a group of people who were concerned at his increasing and almost total power. While there was certainly a wider concern about returning to the bad old days of rule by a king, many of the conspirators were also motivated by personal power and prestige; several of them were related by blood ties and had enormous amounts to gain personally through his removal. One person who had been a close friend of Caesar was portrayed by Shakespeare as a man who betrayed his friend, and so his name has become used as a way of insultingly labelling someone as a disloyal schemer: BRUTUS! Incidentally, Caesar was murdered on a date that in the Roman calendar was described as the Ides of March. This equates to our 15 March. The intriguing explanation to why this is the case is given in more detail in Appendix IV of this book.

Well, I never knew that . . .
. . . Caesar now means emperor, but Caesar wasn't one

Once Caesar was dead, it was not altogether clear what would happen in Rome or who would take power. At one point the Empire was split between Caesar's great-nephew Octavian and one of Julius Caesar's ex-generals Mark Antony. Mark Antony then married Octavian's sister, but quickly abandoned her to become Cleopatra's new lover! Octavian was not amused and eventually there was a battle in Greece which Octavian won. Cleopatra and Mark Antony both escaped and fled back to Egypt, where Cleopatra famously killed herself by the bite of a poisonous snake.

So Octavian became the undisputed Roman leader and in 27 BC became the first ever Roman EMPEROR. He created a new title that referred to the massive reputation of his father and added a new element of regalism, majesty and universal acclaim: CAESAR AUGUSTUS. In fact, from then on all Roman emperors would include the name 'Caesar' in their title, and crowds would tend to chant this name instead of the

emperor's actual name. Hence Roman emperors are collectively called 'THE CAESARS'; and hence too the ironic greeting that is still used nowadays to refer to someone who is, or thinks they are, all-powerful: HAIL CAESAR.

Before Julius Caesar became leader of the Republic of Rome (he was never emperor, as it was a republic, not an empire, at the time), he had a senior government role in which he was responsible, together with other senior figures, for overseeing various changes to the law. Now, the Romans had a term *a matre caesus*, meaning 'cut out of his mother', which described the emergency operation for difficult births of cutting a

mother's abdomen open to remove the baby. However, infection and other factors meant that the survival rates for mother and baby from this operation were very low. There is no evidence that Julius Caesar was born in this way – in fact, his mother lived for another 30 years after his birth, so it is unlikely. However, one of the areas of law that he revised included the introduction of a requirement that such an operation be carried out when a mother was known to be dying so that the baby would be saved. While the name Caesar had a different derivation, the similarity with *caesus* led to the operation being called CAESAREAN SECTION. (In this case the word 'section' means 'cut', as in doing an operation on a live [*viv-*] animal: VIVISECTION.) A different application of the word in law relates to the occasion when someone who may cause damage to themselves or others through mental instability is 'cut out' of society: they may be SECTIONED, that is, forcibly held in custody by applying a specific section of the

Mental Health Act. Of course a segment that is cut out from the whole is called a SECTION. If you *cut across* an object and look at the new surface it is a CROSS-SECTION. From the same root we also get the English name for garden cutters used in pruning (cutting out unwanted stems): SECATEURS.

Kruptein is the old Germanic word meaning hidden. Hence we get the name for rooms, often under churches, where dead bodies are entombed or 'hidden' from view: CRYPT; the kind of word puzzles where the answers are hidden, either through hints that are difficult to unravel – CRYPTIC CLUES – or through jumbled-up letters – CRYPTOGRAMS; and the idea of 'hiding' data or secret meanings within messages: ENCRYPTION. Using the Latin word for writing, *graphein*, we also get the term for hidden writing: CRYPTOGRAPHY.

Cryptology is the science of encrypting (or encoding) messages so that they are unintelligible to others – unless they have the code or cipher to decode it. Prior to cryptology, secret messages were still sent, but the basis of keeping them secret was covering up the fact that there was a message there at all. *Stega* is Latin for 'covered'; hence the dinosaur whose back is covered in large flat plates is called a STEGOSAURUS. Therefore the skill of covering up messages is called STEGANOGRAPHY. Methods of doing this included writing messages on thin silk and then rolling it tightly, covering it in wax and getting the messenger to swallow it. Or a message could be tattooed on a servant's shaven head, after which his hair was allowed to grow. In Ancient China some letters of a message could be written in ink flavoured with mulberry juice. Silkworms would then be attracted to those letters and so a secret message could be gleaned.

In the first century BC, when Julius Caesar was invading Gaul, he needed to send messages that the Gauls (some of whom spoke Latin) could not decode. So the message was first written in Latin, then translated into Greek words – and then the letters were 'shifted' by two places alphabetically (so that, in our alphabet, A would become C, B would become D, etc.) In fact the cipher of using one language translated into another is still called the CAESAR CODE and, when a shift of X places is added it is called the 'CAESAR CODE WITH AN X SHIFT'.

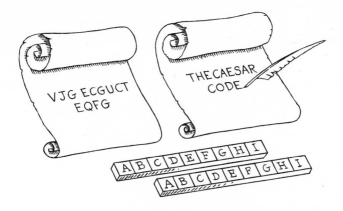

For example, the word 'day' translated into French would be *jour*. Applying a +2 shift would then give LQWT. This would be an English to French Caesar code with a 2 shift.

Another form of cryptology is where the true meaning is only apparent when alternate lines are read: READING BETWEEN THE LINES.

Julius Caesar also created a single-page news sheet called the *Acta Diurna* that was issued daily for a period of time in ancient Rome and stuck to walls around the city. This was the world's first ever NEWSPAPER. **WINKT!**

3

The Rise and Fall of the Roman Empire

During the 300 years after Octavian became the first Roman Emperor, the Roman Empire peaked in its power and its geographical extent. While the western Empire was doomed to an ignoble end, the eastern Empire would last for another thousand years.

Well, I never knew that ...
... Rome was led by an eagle and beaten by a weasel

The Roman emperors were constantly wishing to demonstrate their power and wealth to the rest of the population. One method of doing so was to reserve the use of a particular colour for themselves alone. This colour was in fact very rare and very expensive, as it was only available from a rare shellfish from the area of Turkey near the town of Tyre. The shellfish was called porphura or Tyrian porphura, and the rich reddy-blue colour came to be called *porpura* or, in England, PURPLE. Over several centuries the colour became more widespread as different sources for it were found, but the association with something very special remained – so much so that circles of purple dyed cloth would be sewn on to other clothes and fabrics to make them seem very impressive and to make the wearers appear very successful. From this we get the phrase referring to a very successful period or set of events: a PURPLE PATCH. In fact during the 5th century even soldiers had such patches sewn on to their uniforms.

Jupiter, leader of the Roman gods, used eagles as messengers and to deliver thunderbolts to people he wanted to punish. Therefore early in their history the Romans adopted an eagle holding thunderbolts in its claws as a symbol of their power. Every legion had one emblem of an eagle on a pole that would be protected by the soldiers to the death. The person

who carried this emblem was called the *aquilifer* (Latin for 'eagle-bearer'). The Roman eagle always looked to the right – the lucky side. This emblem was adopted by the Holy Roman Empire of the Middle Ages until it had expanded so far as to cover much of modern Germany, where there was a tradition of a left-looking eagle. Hence the Holy Roman Empire adopted a new symbol: the TWO-HEADED EAGLE, looking both ways. In the 15th century the Czar of Russia, Ivan III, married the daughter of the Holy Roman Emperor and adopted the same symbol. When the Holy Roman Empire collapsed the emerging territories, notably Austria and parts of Germany, retained the symbol as well; so the double-headed eagle symbol is now used in Austria, Germany and Russia. Incidentally, the American bald-headed eagle symbol always looks to the right as well.

In Germany in AD 9 several Roman legions were ambushed and routed by a very cunning early Saxon leader who was named after the old Germanic word for 'weasel', Arminius. As a reminder for the need of vigilance, one of the four main Roman roads in England was named after him: ERMINE

STREET. Incidentally, this is also where we get the name for the white winter fur of a weasel: ERMINE.

In medieval heraldry there were officially only eight backgrounds that could be used. From the Latin word meaning 'to dye', *tingere* (from which we get the words tint and tinge), they were called tinctures. Red, green, blue, black and purple were called the 'colours'. Yellow and white, representing gold and silver, were called the 'metals'. The eighth background was called a 'fur' and was represented as white with a pattern on that notionally represented the shape of a weasel skin, with a head and four legs. Hence in heraldry the eighth background is called ERMINE.

As the Roman Empire grew it took an old Indo-European word, *pag*, which meant 'to fasten', and used a variation of it to describe how two nations 'bound' themselves together by treaty: PAX. This gives us the words for such a deal, PACT, and for the resultant friendship, PEACE. The peace brought about by the Roman Empire was therefore called the PAX ROMANA. This was later copied by the British Empire, which claimed to have brought about the PAX BRITANNICA. From the same root comes the verb meaning to stop fighting or arguing: to PACIFY. Interestingly, some peace treaties required the transfer of monies, and this is the derivation of the verb to PAY money. This word 'pay' was then applied to other skills and aspects of diplomacy and the building of alliances. Hence we get the phrases meaning to listen to someone carefully: to PAY ATTENTION, or to PAY HEED; to acknowledge someone else's status: to PAY RESPECT; to comment on someone else's positive attributes: to PAY A COMPLIMENT; and the act of travelling, originally to see them in their own land as part of making a treaty: TO PAY A VISIT.

The idea of *bonding* planks of wood together in shipbuilding led to the idea of 'paying' them with a sealant such as tar. This was especially important along the seam that went all around the ship at deck level and was called the 'devil'. Hence we get the term meaning that there will be very significant consequences of having not done something, such as a ship sinking because it wasn't watertight! – THE DEVIL TO PAY AND NO HOT PITCH, often shortened to just THE DEVIL TO PAY.

Well, I never knew that . . .
. . . some of the emperors took building the Empire literally

Running such a massive entity as the Roman Empire was not easy, and few emperors really distinguished themselves. Among both the successful and the less than successful there have been several characters who have influenced our view of the Romans and provided us with phrases in our modern language.

The emperor after Augustus was named after the River Tiber that flows through Rome: TIBERIUS. He became so scared of being assassinated that he tried to run the empire from a private palace on the island of Capri! Needless to say it did not work very well!

Tiberius was followed by his great-nephew who became infamous for orgies, killings, incest and other very bad behaviour. In fact, he even demanded that one of his 'best friends' become a senator. What was really bizarre is that this friend was a HORSE! This emperor's name was CALIGULA.

Eventually this madness led to his murder by the army, who then chose a stuttering, apparently bumbling and weak man as the next emperor. In fact he turned out to be more effective than many. His name was CLAUDIUS. Claudius oversaw the expansion of the Empire into Britain and even brought elephants to Britain to scare the natives into submission. On seeing the white cliffs of Dover the Roman invaders used their word for white, *albus* (which also gives us 'albino'), hence giving England one of its traditional names: ALBION.

Claudius was eventually poisoned by his scheming fourth wife, Agrippina, who then made her stepson the next emperor. In AD 64 Rome suffered one of the worst fires in its history. The Emperor, who was mentally unstable, is said to have played his lyre and recited poetry (one of his less harmful vices) while watching his city burn. This story has given us a phrase that has come down through the years to describe someone doing futile and irrelevant things in the face of disaster: TO FIDDLE WHILE ROME BURNS. His name was NERO. Incidentally, Nero blamed the fire on Christians and crucified hundreds of them in one of his private gardens.

He then covered them in oil and set fire to the bodies to provide lighting through the night. Nice! Afterwards Nero claimed much of the ruined city as the grounds for his new 'golden' palace. This proved too much even for the indulgent Romans, and Nero killed himself just before the people killed him.

The next 12 months saw a quick succession of four emperors in a row, each one getting the army to kill the previous one. This period is called the YEAR OF THE FOUR EMPERORS. The last

47

of these was called Vespasian, who wisely decided to distract the army by getting them to build the most colossal gladiatorial arena the world had ever seen. It took several years to build and successfully kept the army busy and out of mischief – such as conducting yet another military coup! The arena itself was named to reflect its size of over 50,000 seats: the COLOSSEUM.

By AD 130 the Roman Empire had extended to the very north of Britain and to the Rhine in Germany. The emperor at the time then decided to stop further expansion and consolidate the lines of defence with various structures, perhaps the most famous of which is a wall all the way across the north of Britain from Carlisle on the west coast to Sunderland on the east coast. The emperor's name was HADRIAN and the wall was HADRIAN'S WALL. In fact this marked the northernmost reach of the Roman Empire, which at this point had over 100 million people under its control and extended from Hadrian's Wall in the north to Egypt in the south, and from the Atlantic Ocean off the coast of Spain to Babylon and the Dead Sea in the east.

Incidentally, the Latin word for 'outlying' was *limus* (from which we get the word LIMIT), and so the extreme borders of the empire, such as Hadrian's Wall, were called *limes*. Given the English habit of adding silent letter 'b's to words, as in 'thumb' and 'lamb', the English word for an outlying part of a human body or a tree came to be LIMB. The idea of being on a risky outlying part of a tree where branches are thin gives us the phrase to be OUT ON A LIMB. Also, the part of the afterlife where souls wait before their fate is decided is LIMBO. This gives us the phrase meaning to be waiting for an outcome: TO BE IN LIMBO.

Interestingly, before he became emperor, Hadrian used go to the baths with his soldiers. One day he saw a soldier scraping himself with a piece of broken pot because he could not afford  the correct item, called a *strigil*, so he arranged for the soldier to receive some extra money. The next time he returned to the baths he saw many more soldiers using broken pots and trying to get his attention. In exasperation he said, 'Keep scraping with your pots – you will not scrape an acquaintance with me!' Hence the phrase TO SCRAPE AN ACQUAINTANCE, meaning to apply cunning to get to know someone and so receive favours.

Well, I never knew that . . .
. . . the capital of the Roman Empire wasn't always Rome

During the 3rd century AD tribes called the Slavs, who were relatively peaceful peoples living in central and eastern

Europe, began to be forced westwards by encroaching invaders from the Russian steppes. This forced them up against the warlike Germanic tribes. They did not fare well in this clash, and the Germanic tribes would often sell them on as prisoners to the declining Roman Empire, which was desperate for manpower. These people would then be sent around the Empire for service in various military and civil projects. Their name became used as a derisory term for weak people who did menial jobs: SLAVES. Incidentally, these people also gave their name to central European countries, such as SLOVAKIA, SLOVENIA and YUGOSLAVIA.

Despite Hadrian's attempts to consolidate, the Empire was already too big to manage and over the next 100 years things started to go wrong. Political turmoil was rife and in the period of just 50 years from AD 235 there were no fewer than 18 different emperors.

During the 3rd century a city in the far east of the Empire gradually became the administrative centre for that part of Rome's dominions. Then in AD 330 the new Roman emperor,

Constantine, made it the capital of the eastern half of the Empire and renamed it after himself by adding the Greek word for city, *polis*, to his name: CONSTANTINOPLE. Later it was renamed again, as Byzantium, and the eastern Roman Empire, ruled from this city, became known as the BYZANTINE EMPIRE. Later still, the city was renamed again, becoming – as it remains today – ISTANBUL.

During his reign Constantine was unusually benevolent to Christians, and shortly before his death he decided to become the first officially Christian emperor and to make Christianity the official religion of the Empire. In fact he also revised the gospels and reissued them across the Empire. When some people refused to follow the new scriptures, preferring to stick with what they had before, they were labelled using the word *haeriticus*, meaning choice. This was then used as a criticism against people who were choosing not to accept any official doctrine: they were called HERETICS.

Procopius was an adviser to the Byzantine emperor Justinian around AD 550. He had access to many secrets and recorded many of them, describing who said or did what and when. He hid these documents and labelled them using the Greek word for secret – *anecdota*, from which we get our word meaning a story about something: ANECDOTE.

By the 5th century the Roman Empire had split into two parts, the eastern Empire ruled from Constantinople and the western Empire ruled from Rome. However, the western Empire was in serious decline, suffering from barbarian attacks, rebellions from its provinces and corruption at all levels in its government. At the beginning of the century these pressures led to the legions being withdrawn from Britain to help defend Rome. This left a power vacuum in Britain that in turn led to invasions by the Angles and Saxons and the emergence of British heroes, such as Hereward the Wake in the Lake District and King Arthur in the south-west, who provided some defence against the flood of foreign invaders.

As increasingly warlike tribes from the steppes of China (such as the Huns, later to be led by Attila) gradually moved west and steadily displaced local tribes, these in turn forced others to move west. Ultimately, several tribes in Germany were forced up to the boundary of the Roman Empire on the River Rhine. For centuries these tribes had been kept in check by the Romans, but as internal politics and other issues weakened the Empire, the pressure on the tribes to move steadily increased. Then in the winter of AD 406 the Rhine froze and the tribes poured over, burst through the imperial defences and marched on Rome itself. The name of one of these tribes has come down through history as a modern word to describe anyone who wantonly destroys civilization. They invaded through what are now France and Spain as far as North Africa, where they took control of the ancient city of Carthage in modern-day Tunisia. From here they attacked and sacked Rome in AD 451. Their destruction of everything that the Romans had stood for led to their name being used in future centuries as a byword for vicious and destructive behaviour. They were the VANDALS.

Several other tribes also roamed across the Roman Empire, and in fact 50 years earlier in AD 402 the emperor was forced to flee Rome in the face of an attack led by Alaric, King of the

Goths, who then destroyed the city. Seven hundred years later a new style of architecture emerged in central Europe with radical new features, including pointed arches and flying buttresses, which were in stark contrast to the previous classical style of 'Romanesque' architecture based upon Roman and Greek temple design. This new architecture was reviled by many architects and masons who claimed it would destroy the beauty and classic lines of religious buildings, and so they named the new style after the warriors who had literally destroyed the physical architecture of the temples in ancient Rome, calling it the GOTHIC STYLE.

In the middle of the 5th century Attila, leader of the Huns, attacked first the eastern and then the western Roman Empire. He received massive bribes to go away, but it was only in AD 457 AD that a remarkable alliance of Romans and barbarians eventually defeated him and forced him to retreat. Ironically, having been the scourge of Europe for many years, he eventually died during a feast from, of all things, a NOSEBLEED! This was caused by his excessive drinking of a very strong home-distilled drink that had the effect of thinning his blood so much that it would not clot!

Many centuries later the outrageous German invasion of Europe in the First World War was compared to Attila's attacks, and so the Germans gained the nickname of THE HUN. Interestingly, though, some central European people felt that Attila had rescued them from the oppressive Roman Empire and various other dictators; so in these countries Attila was seen as a hero. In fact, Attila has been a popular name in a country that named itself after these wild horsemen by combining the word 'Hun' with the term for the ruling ten tribes, *on-ogur*: HUNGARY.

Eventually the last emperor of Rome was caught by a Gothic army but was deemed to be so unimportant that the usual execution of the enemy's leader – in order to prevent any future resurgence – was considered unnecessary. In fact, he was allowed to go and live on an island off the coast of Italy, where he eventually died of old age. Ironically, he had called himself by two of the most prestigious names from Rome's history: ROMULUS AUGUSTUS. Records would suggest that the world did not care or even notice. A surprisingly ignoble end to what had been one of the greatest empires of all time!

Now, the Romans had always been proud to have brought the 'light' of civilization to previously barbaric lands, and more recently as a Christian empire had spread the candle (representing Jesus Christ) of Christianity. With the light of the Roman civilized world  extinguished by barbarian invaders, in the West at least, the ensuing period in Europe became known somewhat poetically as the DARK AGES. **WINKT!**

4

All Roads Lead to Rome and Railways Come from It!

The Roman armies were famous for
their efficiency in road-building –
but did you know that they even laid
tracks for the railways and helped
design the space shuttle?

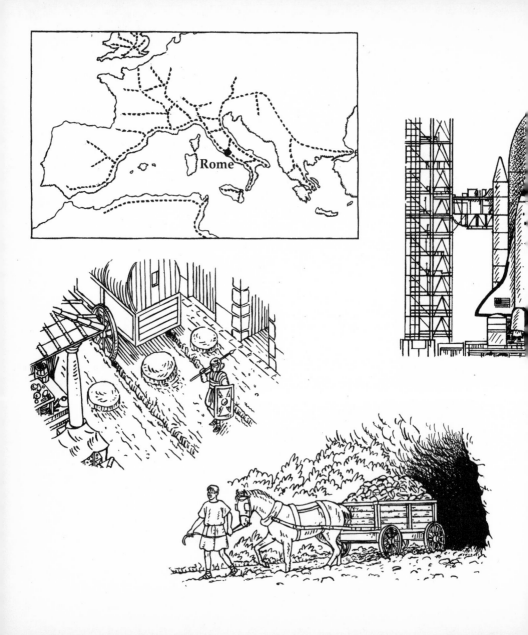

'Well, I never knew that . . .
. . . the Roman army helped design modern railways
and the space shuttle!

In the days of the Roman Empire the roads provided the fastest communication the world had ever seen. In fact at its height there were over 50,000 miles of roads across the Empire.

Their roads were straight and well-maintained, and had stables at regular intervals where riders could exchange horses or relay message to other riders. While each province would have local hubs where roads came together (for example, Londinium in Britain), Rome was the hub of all

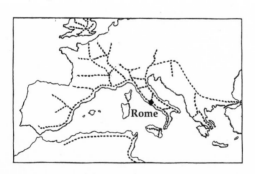

hubs: hence the phrase – which was in fact true – ALL ROADS LEAD TO ROME. Or, as the late comedian W. C. Fields said, 'All roads lead to rum!!!' It was not until the days of the Pony Express in the western United States that such speeds were again achieved as a matter of routine.

The main streets in Rome were paved, with much of central Rome also having underground sewage pipes. However, the poorer areas had basic mud back-streets, where the tenements on either side tipped their sewage straight into the road. This in turn required stepping stones to be introduced so that citizens could at least cross the roads in the winter without stepping in the effluent. To enable access by carts, the

gaps between these stepping stones were standardized and specified by law. Over time this led to carts adopting standard widths between wheels, and this standard was adopted by the Roman army. This in turn meant that when a fully paved road was too expensive, two rows of paving stones set at the correct distance apart could provide a paved route just for the wheels of Roman carts. When the Romans invaded Britain they brought these standard-gauge carts with them, and when they started hauling the tin out of the tin mines in Cornwall, grooves developed in the mud that matched the Roman gauge.

By the 17th century wooden and then metal rails were introduced to make it easier to pull trucks full of tin out of the mines. Naturally these followed the existing ruts, and the new trucks designed to run on them had the same gauge as the old wooden carts. Before long the metal tracks were being extended from the mines to the nearest river or sea port. Now, traditionally main roads between towns tended to follow high ground to avoid marshes and boggy conditions in bad weather. Hence they were called HIGHWAYS, even if over time they sometimes followed old Roman roads that were well drained and lower. Therefore, the mine routes were referred to

as 'highways of metal rails', often shortened to RAILWAYS, even though at this stage, the mining trucks were still pulled by horses.

During the 18th and 19th centuries big stationary steam engines were introduced in the mines in Cornwall and the north of England. Soon the power was also being used to pull the carts up from below, still using the same old rails.

In 1824 the mine owners around Darlington in the north of England decided to build a horse-drawn 'railway' from their mines to the nearest town on a river, Stockton-on-Tees. They had calculated that each horse could pull ten times more coal on rails than it could on a road. However, an 'engine-wright' – steam-engine expert – said that a moving steam engine would be worth 'fifty horses'. He won his argument and went on to create the now famous STOCKTON-ON-TEES TO DARLINGTON RAILWAY. Five years later he won a competition by designing and building the world's fastest train, which was appropriately named *THE ROCKET*! His name was GEORGE STEPHENSON. Incidentally, it is this famous George who has

given his name to people from his birthplace, Newcastle –
GEORDIES.

Stephenson designed the gap between the rails to match the
existing gauge used in the nearby Killingworth Colliery, which
had itself evolved from the tracks used by the Roman mine
carts. This distance subsequently had an extra half an inch
added to allow a little play for manufacturing accuracy. Then,
at 4 feet and $8\frac{1}{2}$ inches, the gauge was standardized by Act of
Parliament to ensure that railways across Britain could be
easily linked together. Hence the name given to the width
between rails still used today in the United Kingdom:
STANDARD GAUGE – and the rest, as they say, is history.

Some very curvy mountain-based railways did have a
narrower gauge as this made the construction of the line
easier. There was even an attempt to introduce a wider-gauge
railway in the 19th century. In fact, for several years the main
lines in England had three rails, with the standard-gauge
trains using the inner rail and the central rail, and the wide-
gauge trains using the inner rail and the outer one. However,

the confusion and immense inefficiency caused by having two gauges of locomotives and carriages, and the horrendously complicated points, led to a re-standardization of the old measurement – the one first developed to cope with Roman sewage. So, incredible as it sounds, the modern British railway gauge derives from ancient Roman sewage! Perhaps that explains the quality of service?

But even that is not the end of the story.

Britain led the world in locomotive and railway design and before long its designs were spreading around the world.

In fact to this day over 60% of all railway tracks in the world (including most of those in France, Germany, Italy, China, Japan and Scandinavia) conform to this same standard gauge.

In 1831 a British locomotive called the *John Bull* was bought and used on the brand new New York to Philadelphia railway in the USA. The gauge of the railway lines was of course the British standard. By the time of the American Civil War in the 1860s various other gauges had been tried, especially in the southern states. However, most of the northern states had decided on the British standard, and so when they won the Civil War this standard was then applied across the USA.

Now, the maximum width of locomotives and carriages themselves had been set in the UK by the distance between adjacent tracks, to ensure that trains could pass each other safely. In the USA the tracks were laid further apart and so the rolling stock was wider and bigger, although the size was limited by the stability based upon the same distance of 4 feet $8\frac{1}{2}$ inches between the wheels. Tunnels in the USA were therefore built to accommodate this maximum size of stable trains.

A century and a half after the Civil War, the company Thiokol, based in Utah, won the contract to manufacture and then service the reusable side Solid Rocket Boosters (SRBs) used on the Space Shuttle. These would be taken to and from Cape Canaveral in Florida by train, and so the maximum size of the rockets (allowing for their protective casings etc.) was determined by the size of the tunnels on the route – which is why, to this day, the SRBs are just over 12 feet in diameter!

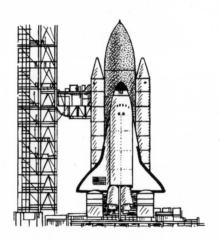

So did the Roman army really help specify the space shuttle? Well, as Julius Caesar would have said, 'Quod erat demonstrandum' (meaning 'which has been demonstrated') – or, as we know it, QED.

Well, I never knew that . . .
. . . so much training has come from a medieval fashion!

The vulgar Latin word for 'pull' was *traginare*. By the Middle Ages the derivate word *trayne* was being used to describe the long clothes that dragged (or were pulled) behind lords and ladies. We know it as TRAIN. In fact, such clothes were very strictly regulated according to status, and there were strict rules as to how long a trayne each noble and his lady could have, depending on their seniority and whether or not they were permitted to have someone holding it for them out of the mud! By the Renaissance period the word had been applied to the sycophantic followers of kings whom they tended to 'pull' around with them, giving us the phrase TRAIN OF ADMIRERS – or, for that matter, TRAIN OF MOURNERS. The word then began to be used more loosely for any such set of things that followed one another. A line of pack mules would be a TRAIN OF MULES; a line of wagons a WAGON TRAIN. Even a sequence of ideas was called a TRAIN OF THOUGHT, and a sequence of linked situations a TRAIN OF EVENTS. So in the 1820s, when engineers first discovered a way of pulling several connected carriages, it is not surprising that they were called a TRAIN OF CARRIAGES. Subsequently this was applied to the whole collection of items including the engine: a TRAIN.

Incidentally, the style of teaching adopted in the Middle Ages emulated the classical idea of 'drawing out' (*educere* in Latin) ideas. Hence our word EDUCATION. Similarly the idea of 'pulling out' ideas and learning gives us the term TRAINING.

Well, I never knew that . . .
. . . a cotton gin has nothing to do with tonic

Shortly after the defeat of Napoleon at Waterloo in 1815, steam engines, which up until this point were very large and used in static positions such as at mines, were becoming sufficiently advanced to be used on mobile platforms. George Stephenson built an engine named after the Prussian saviour of the Battle of Waterloo, *BLÜCHER,* and then another that he named using the Latin word for movement, *motus* (closely related to our words 'motion' and 'motivation') and the word for position, *locus* (which gives us 'location' and 'locality'). The name he used was LOCOMOTION, which has subsequently given us the term for moving steam engines: LOCOMOTIVES. Incidentally, a similar-sounding word for someone who is mad comes from a totally different source – in fact, from an old Arabic word meaning a madman, *al lauqa*, which we know through the Spanish, who adopted it when they were conquered by the Moors in the early Middle Ages – LOCO.

But why is a locomotive also called a steam 'engine'? Interestingly, the Romans gave us many words from the word *genus*, meaning 'birth'. Hence we get the name for the first book of the Bible, which describes the birth of the world: GENESIS. To give birth to something is to GENERATE it. Inherited characteristics that we get through our birth are the result of GENES and GENETICS. The study of the history of who was born to whom is GENEALOGY. Something that applies to all the people in a tribe who are genetically related is GENERIC or GENERAL. A military leader, originally of a tribe who were all related through birth, is a GENERAL. The parts of human bodies that are involved in producing the birth of the next GENERATION are GENITALS. People who are part of the same clan/family care for each other and tend to be GENTLE with each other. Someone who shows such courtesies beyond their family or clan is called a GENTLEMAN and courteous social behaviour is GENTEEL. Someone who has inborn skills inherited from birth is a GENIUS or INGENIOUS. A mechanism made by someone with such skills is called an ENGINE. Someone who makes such things is an ENGINEER. When the engines became steam-powered they were called STEAM ENGINES. When these steam engines were used to make machinery that processed cotton, the whole mechanism was called a COTTON GIN – short for cotton engine. **WINKT!**

5

Rome at War

The Roman army was expert at pitching its tents and even became the first 'camping' champions. The trouble was, if they became drunk on duty they were *really* stoned!

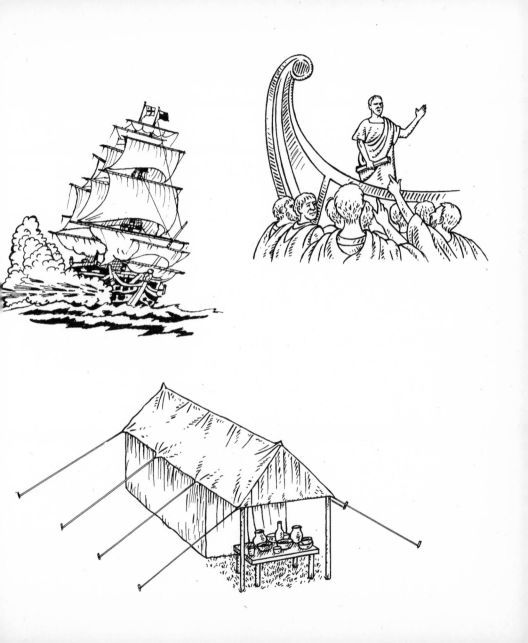

Well, I never knew that . . .
. . . the Roman army subsided when it wasn't needed

During the Republic, Romans were terrified of military coups and so Roman armies were always commanded by *two* generals. On the basis that these generals needed to consult with each other and with the Senate back in Rome they were called military CONSULS. In fact, each one would take control on alternate days to ensure that neither could make any concerted move against the State. This led to silly games being played by the consuls, who were essentially politically ambitious rich young men wanting to get publicity, rather than experienced fighters skilled at winning battles. For example, one consul might set up his army in a weak position so that when the other consul took control the next day he would be unable to mount a successful attack and claim the glory!

This is why the Roman army developed a superb command and control structure that if necessary could ignore potentially disastrous orders from bad generals but respond very well to skilful ones such as Julius Caesar. The key officer in all of this was the commander of a unit of theoretically 100 men, although usually only 80 men in practice: the CENTURION. The root of this word was *cent-*, meaning 100, which also gave us the words for 100 years, CENTURY, a 100th of a dollar, CENT, and a crawling creature that looks as if it has 100 legs, CENTIPEDE.

The Roman army was very well organized, to such an extent that the reserves and auxiliary support troops of the army would be kept fresh by sitting down until they were needed. Hence they were called *subsidii*, from the Latin word *subsidere*, meaning sitting down. Hence we get the word for something that goes down: SUBSIDE. Over many hundreds of years a version of the word evolved to describe grants of money kept *in reserve* and then issued by the King and, later, Parliament: SUBSIDY. Another word developed to describe a semi-independent or auxiliary part of a larger corporation: SUBSIDIARY.

The Latin word *monere*, meaning to advise, was used to describe the officer who instructed new recruits in the rules of the Roman army and ensured that they followed them. From here the word came to be used to describe the slave whose duty it was to rouse a household in the morning and attend to the basic chores such as lighting a fire, etc. Hence the same word is now used to describe schoolchildren who are given extra responsibilities at school: MONITOR.

Roman soldiers typically marched 20 miles each day before stopping and building a temporary fort for protection at night. This distance became accepted as the amount of ground that someone travelling on foot could be expected to cover each day. In fact, even in the Middle Ages it was used as a guideline for awarding towns the charters that gave them the right to hold fairs. These were important ways of attracting people from afar, generating trade and therefore income for a town. On the basis that a man could walk 20 miles in a day it was considered reasonable that he could walk one-third of that distance to a fair, spend one-third of a day there and then walk back for the last third of the day. Hence charters were not awarded within $6\frac{2}{3}$ miles of another town that already had a charter. Incidentally, the Latin word for festival days was *feriae*, from which we get the word FAIR.

Armies on the march would have to stop at night and often set up tents in open fields. Over time these collections of tents became known by the word for 'open field', which nowadays is used for a group of buildings over a large area: CAMPUS. From this word we get the term for a collection of military tents: a CAMP. On the day of a battle each army would sometimes offer up one fighter from its camp to challenge the best fighter from the other camp. These fights might be just a warm-up for the main battle, but sometimes they would replace the full battle and all the associated loss of life, with the side whose fighter was defeated accepting defeat and

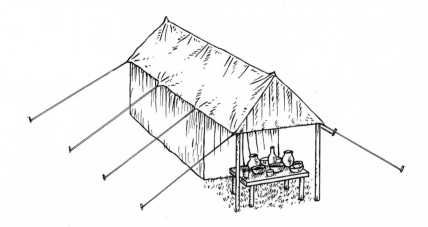

walking away from the battlefield. These fighters chosen from the best men of each camp were called CAMPIONS or, as we know them, CHAMPIONS.

Incidentally, the Dutch word for camp is *leger* and the Dutch word for around is *be*. From this, the Dutch created a word to describe the situation of an army or town that is besieged and has enemy troops camped all around them: *be-legeren* or, as we use it, BELEAGUERED.

Roman legions always marched with thousands of stakes (*pales* in Latin) so that every night they could create their own protective fort. In enemy territory the stakes were placed at the top of earth ramparts dug by the soldiers to improve the defences further. As we have seen, this gave us the word PALISADE. The hole left after the soil was removed also formed a defensive ditch in front of the walls. One of these palisaded ramparts was called a *vallum*. From this we get our words VALLEY and VALE, linked to the ditch. Over time, the word *vallis* (actually referring to the stakes) evolved to give us our word WALL. On board medieval ships there were 'walls' of wood

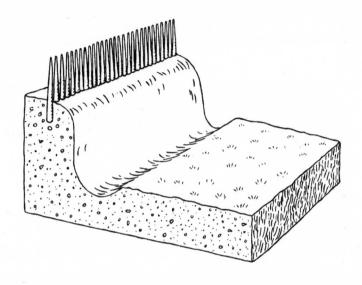

around the top of the deck to give protection to the crew. As this is where the early medieval guns were located, they became known as GUNWALES, usually pronounced 'GUNNELS'. As these gunwales represent the very top of the hull, they indicated an absolute maximum level at which cargo could be carried. Hence the phrase meaning loaded to absolute maximum capacity: LOADED TO THE GUNNELS. In naval parlance this can also mean being drunk, based upon having personally taken on board a maximum cargo of booze!

Well, I never knew that . . .
. . . it helps to speak from a beak

Foris is the Roman word meaning outside. Hence someone who comes from outside your own country is a FOREIGNER, and the woods that covered much of Europe outside towns and cities were called FORESTS.

Roman orators found that an excellent place to state their views and kick off any important debate was the central marketplace, where there was a ready potential audience available of bored shoppers and stallholders. We still use the Roman name for an outside (*foris*) marketplace in this sense of somewhere to express one's views and debate them with others: a FORUM.

In the ancient world, war galleys were equipped with high prows for defence and bronze rams for smashing into enemy ships. These were described by Romans as 'beaks' (or, in Latin, *rostra*). Around 340 BC a Roman consul named Maenius was sent from Rome to clean up an area of the coast near modern-day Anzio that had become infamous for pirates. The expedition was very successful, killing many pirates and bringing others back as slaves. The ships were destroyed and the fronts of some of these vessels were taken back to Rome and set up in the marketplace (*forum*) as a publicity stunt to show how successful the expedition had been, and to reinforce the power and capability of the government. The forum was already used by people who wanted to speak publicly on matters important to them (just like Speakers' Corner in Hyde Park today), and these additions not only added colour but also became popular higher points for people to use to speak from: thus we get the word  ROSTRUM. Incidentally, the word *rostra*, meaning 'beak', itself derived from the word *rodere*, meaning 'to gnaw'. Other words from this source are those meaning to gnaw away chemically: CORRODE; to be gnawed at by the elements: ERODED; and an animal that gnaws almost constantly: a RODENT.

The Romans called their fighting ships 'galleys'. These were equipped with detachable masts and sails, for use when travelling from port to port, as well as with oars for manoeuvring in battle (this was because if a mast was up when a ship was ramming an enemy, it was likely to topple over and sink its own ship!). Many centuries later, when cannons fired with gunpowder were introduced, there was less need to ram enemy ships to sink them, and so masts became taller and permanent. Travel across the rough seas of the Atlantic also meant that holes for oars were impractical, and so by the late 16th century few ships still had oars. To differentiate the new breed of ship they were called GALLEONS.

Roman soldiers initially used large round shields similar to those used by Greeks. The army then evolved a larger oval shield called a *scutum*. Kings, generals and other important people would have their shields carried for them by trusted friends from the nobility. This role took a name derived from the shield – *scutari*. Many years later the role and title were re-established in the Middle Ages, and subsequently the title was seen as conveying a status between that of a nobleman and a gentlemen and was used to describe assistants to knights: SQUIRES.

Because they served the most senior members of the army mounted on horses, squires were strongly involved with horses, and this led to the Latin word for horse, *equus*, becoming associated with the role of squire. This link led in two directions. The first connection was to the role of the person who looked after the king's horses, subsequently developing to include providing other personal services to members of the royal family and their horses: EQUERRY – a role still in use today. The other was to a title that became associated with men such as knights and sons of nobles who held property in their own right: ESQUIRE. During the 19th and 20th centuries this was often shortened to ESQ., and would often appear on envelopes of letters written to people who owned their own property.

Well, I never knew that . . .
. . . 'one in ten' for the Romans was worse than a steep hill

The Romans organized everything according to the number ten and multiples of it. As well as the army officers who commanded a hundred men (centurions) there were non-commissioned officers who looked after ten men each (often eight in practice) called *decurions*. These men, especially the centurions, were the bedrock of the army and provided the deep battle experience to ensure the men fought professionally and bravely.

The Romans defined the distance of 1,000 paces (easy for soldiers to count) using the Latin word for a thousand, *mille*, or, as we know it, MILE. They even built castles every mile along Hadrian's Wall: MILECASTLES.

In fact, they even used the number 10 when they killed themselves! When a Roman unit mutinied, or refused to follow orders, those involved would be forced to line up and draw a bead out of a sack. One in ten of the beads was coloured. Everyone who drew a coloured bead would then be stripped naked and their colleagues would then be forced to throw jagged rocks at them until they were dead. This was called decimation – from where we get the term for a slaughter: DECIMATED.

The Latin word *picca* was used to describe a very long spear that we would know as a PIKE. The same derivation gives us the name of a long pointy fish with sharp dangerous teeth – PIKE – and also a sharp point often used on fencing or railings: SPIKE. A variant of the word was also used to describe sticking long poles into the ground to set up army tents, giving us the phrase to PITCH A TENT. The idea that these tents would have sloping roofs, both for convenience and also to allow rain to flow away easily, gives us the sense of the word to describe the angle of a roof: THE PITCH OF A ROOF.

The idea was also applied to setting up tents or covers for market stalls, and so the area for a market stall is called a PITCH, and the process of setting out your wares (literally or metaphorically) to attract customers is called your SALES PITCH.

The idea of thrusting an object towards someone else, as a soldier would thrust his pike, gives us the sense of PITCHING A BALL, for example in baseball.

The original word *picca* also gives us the words for a farming implement used for piercing and moving hay: a PITCHFORK; and a digging tool that resembles a giant axe but that actually has a pointed end rather than a blade to help it penetrate hard ground: a PICK-AXE.

The Romans constantly stole military technology from their enemies – usually killing them first, of course. Their soldiers first looked like Greek soldiers, with round bronze shields called *hoplons*. These soldiers were called HOPLITES. Breast-plates and helmets with flexible cheek plates were gradually adopted, together with Celtic-style shields that were bigger and lighter – and eventually were curved too, giving us the classic Roman shield. Their throwing spears (*pila*) were copied from heavy Spanish throwing spears, with extra lead added to make them even more punchy. They were even designed to bend on impact so that they could not be thrown back!

Hortus was a Latin word for an enclosure, which is in fact the origin of the word for nurturing plants in an enclosed area: HORTICULTURE. It was also used for the part of a Roman army camp where the soldiers came together (*co-* in Latin) to practise. Hence the area, then the unit of soldiers itself, was called *co-hortus* – or, as we know the term, COHORT. A cohort would be a substantial number of men, around 500, and we we have come to use the word to mean a lot of people in some kind of organized form: COHORTS of people. Incidentally, the term for the area of the camp (*cohortus*) was subsequently used to describe the main open area in a castle, giving us the term COURTYARD.

A Roman legion would consist of ten cohorts – nearly 5,000 highly trained and well-equipped men – and would be an awe-inspiring sight. Hence the term for a large number of intimidating and potentially overwhelming people: LEGIONS. **WINKT!**

6

Roman Gods and Superstitions

The Romans based much of their religion on the Greek gods, and added some of their own for good measure – which gave them a lot to be superstitious about!

Well, I never knew that . . .
. . . bacchanalian parties could turn grotesque

The Romans were an incredibly pragmatic bunch. If they came across something that worked better than what they already had, they would take the idea and improve upon it. Indeed, they would steal just about anything that wasn't nailed to the floor (they probably even stole the idea of nails!). For example, they stole the Greek gods and renamed them. Thus Ares, the Greek god of war, became MARS, and even the god of gods, Zeus, became JUPITER, and so on. Among other things, they even stole the best Greek stories, such as 'The Twelve Tasks of Heracles'. He was renamed HERCULES, but the tasks remained the same. Hence we get a term for an extremely difficult task: A HERCULEAN CHALLENGE/TASK.

The Roman god Bacchus discovered how to make wine from grapes and shared this secret with mortal men. An annual festival to Bacchus was held on 16 and 17 March. Over time it became more and more debauched, until it was too much for even the Romans to stomach (and that is saying something!). It was officially banned in 186 BC. Hence his name has become associated with the debauched and drunken orgies of Rome, giving us the word meaning drunken and orgiastic: BACCHANALIAN.

The cult of Bacchus was then forced to continue in secret and in many cases literally to go underground in Rome, the devotees using grottoes and underground caves for their worship of the god. Many such secret places were decorated with pictures and carvings of orgies and scary demons. When some of these were discovered 500 years ago they were described as *pittura grotesca*, meaning cave painting, which has led to a new English word meaning very unpleasant: GROTESQUE. This word is also the source of a shortened version that tends to mean dirty or unpleasant: GROTTY.

Os and *or* are two versions of the same Latin word that means 'mouth' or 'little face'. In vineyards small discs showing the face of Bacchus, god of wine, were hung up to win the god's support for a good harvest. These 'little faces' that would be blown around in the wind were known as oscillium, from which we get the word OSCILLATE. A priest who acts as the mouth of the gods is an ORACLE. Using one's mouth to win over an audience is called ORATORY.

In ancient Rome many temples were adorned with statues of gods, several of whom would be depicted seated – for example, Minerva (upon whom the Britannia figure on UK coins is based). When people came to seek guidance or help from the gods they would give a donation to the priests and then leave a question or message, scratched on either a wax tablet or a thin lead sheet, which the priest would then place on the lap of the statue for the deity's consideration. The priest would then return and say that 'the matter is now IN THE LAP OF THE GODS'.

The Romans had a goddess of nature, fertility and hunting. She supposedly shone with vitality and health in addition to being immortal, and so was called 'The Shining One' or in

Latin Diviana. We know her better by a name that has become popular for girls: DIANA.

The Roman goddess of female passion had a name from which we get a word for passion and sexual arousal : STIMULA, giving us STIMULATE.

There were three immortal sisters whose job it was to torment wrongdoers when they were sent to hell. These sisters were always strongly focused upon particular people and particular situations, and so their name has come into use in our language to describe someone's feelings and actions when they are incensed by a misdeed. The sisters were called the FURIES, from where we get the word FURIOUS.

Well, I never knew that . . .
. . . thirty women kept Rome's fire burning

Legend has it that Romulus was the son of the god of war, Mars, and a princess who became a priestess to Vesta, the goddess of the hearth. In Vesta's honour the Romans built a temple in the centre of Rome. Carefully selected maidens were installed there and dedicated thirty years of their lives to looking after the holy fire in the hearth of the temple. These women were called the VESTAL VIRGINS. If they were found to have lost their virginity, or if they failed to keep Vesta's flame alight, they were killed by being buried alive. This was because of the Romans' belief that if the flame went out then Rome would fall – a bit like the rumour that if the ravens leave the Tower of London then London will fall, which is of course why their wings are clipped!

The goddess of death was called Morta, from which we get the French word for death, *mort,* and the term for someone who deals with dead bodies, MORTICIAN. From the same root we get the concept of a large loan that the borrower pledges (gages) to repay before they die: MORTGAGE.

The Roman god of the underworld was called Orcus. He was fierce and often depicted as ugly, always as dangerous. His name gives us the word for a giant goblin, OGRE, and J. R. R. Tolkien used it in his book *Lord of the Rings* as the basis for the name of his evil perverted elves: ORCS. The scariest and biggest predators in the world are killer whales, also known as ORCAS.

The Greek goddess of chance was called Tyche as in 'YOU LUCKY TYCHE!' The Roman goddess of good luck was called Fortuna, and her symbol was a spinning wheel, representing the random events and ever-turning course of life. From her we get the word meaning lucky, FORTUNATE, and the word for significant wealth, a FORTUNE. We also get an old expression that has been used as the name of a TV quiz show: the WHEEL OF FORTUNE.

The father of the Roman gods and the direct equivalent of the Greek god Zeus was known as 'The Shining Father' or Dies Pater – better known to us as JUPITER. He was also known as Jove. As the leader of the Roman gods he was depicted as a powerful, confident and happy god, and so anyone who exhibited this behaviour was called JOVIAL. As he was the most important God his name was used for the largest planet in our solar system: JUPITER.

Mars was the god of war, and so anything associated with war is called MARTIAL. Reinterpreted over time, this gives us the title of a king's military planner, MARSHAL, and, via French, the word for how soldiers travel to war, MARCH, and also the English name of the Roman month named after the god, MARCH.

One of the early Roman gods, Terminus, was designated the god of boundaries and endings. Stones bearing his name and that of the owner were placed at the edge of a person's property as a clear delineator of ownership. People believed that if anyone moved such a stone in an attempt to take the land then the god would kill them; hence TERMINATED. His name has subsequently been associated with the end of various things, including journeys, so that, for example central London railway stations are called TERMINI and illnesses that prove fatal are TERMINAL.

Cupid was the son of Venus, goddess of beauty and love, and one of her many lovers, the god Mercury, the flying messenger of the gods. Not surprisingly, Cupid's abilities

included flying and making people fall in love. However, he was embarrassed by the fact that his mother had so many affairs. He therefore had the god of silence cast a spell upon a rose such that when he touched one of his mum's lovers it would prevent them from speaking of their liaison. From this legend arose a link between roses and secrecy that became widespread during the later Middle Ages. Hence the Latin phrase for a secret: SUB ROSA, meaning 'under the rose'; also the tradition of carving roses into the ceilings of Roman Catholic confessionals and banqueting rooms to remind people that anything said there in the spirit of the moment must still be considered confidential. This is also why central embossed decorations on ceilings are called CEILING ROSES – even if they are no longer in the shape of a rose!

Being the goddess of love and passion, Venus has also given her name to illnesses that can result from related activities. VENEREAL DISEASES or VD.

The Romans referred to sacrificial animals, which clearly had no chance of escape, by a word that we use for people who are picked on for some reason and suffer significant consequences: VICTIM (from *victima*).

Well, I never knew that . . .
. . . a pedant is never sinister

Like the Greeks, the Romans imagined that certain stars could be joined by lines to make the shapes of animals. One such grouping made the shape of a dog. The brightest star in this group was in fact one of the brightest stars in the night sky and was named Sirius after the dog-headed Egyptian god Osiris. The collection of stars was called Canis Major or the Great Dog. The Romans observed that during the hottest days of the summer Sirius rose and set with the sun. They concluded that this conjunction meant that the combined heat of Sirius and the sun created the extra heat experienced, and called this period caniculares dies: THE DOG DAYS OF SUMMER. Incidentally, in 1975 Al Pacino starred in a film called *Dog Day Afternoon*, about incompetent bank robbers during this very hot part of the summer. It was based on a true story.

Incidentally, the association of hot, lazy afternoons with 'dog days' subsequently led to the short watches on board

Royal Navy ships between 4 p.m. and 8 p.m., the period that included teatime and relaxing, being called the DOG WATCHES.

The Romans believed strongly in the influence of the stars upon their daily lives. However, some of the star signs that they inherited from the Greeks are different from those that we use today. Notably, their 8th sign was called Ophiucus and represented a snake. This name is still used by astronomers to describe that star system in the night sky. The Greek constellation of Scorpio was larger than we currently recognize it, and the Romans reinterpreted the shape, redrawing the claws of the scorpion and in so doing freeing up some stars. These they redrew as a pair of scales, thus creating the new star sign LIBRA. However, they wished to retain only 12 signs in total and so they stopped using the snake sign – leaving us with our modern set of 12 zodiac signs.

The Romans believed that the goddess Night had three children: Clotho, Lacesis and Atropos. Collectively they determined people's lives by spinning the threads of life, measuring them, and then cutting them. The collective name for these deities has given us the word meaning a pre-determined future: THE FATES. Hence the expression IN THE HANDS OF FATE, or originally YOUR LIFE IS IN THE HANDS OF THE FATES.

The ancients believed that there were four fluids or humours within humans that dictated your level of health, happiness and general well-being. These were blood, phlegm, bile and black bile. When these were all in a good balance then the person would be in good HUMOUR.

Greeks and Romans also believed that there were four elements or essences that made up the world. These were earth, fire, air and water. However, some believed that there was a fifth that somehow bound the other four together and provided a higher level of being. This vital and much sought after elixir was called the fifth (*quint*) essence, giving us our word for the key element of something: QUINTESSENTIAL.

Many cultures have believed that there are two spirits in all of us – a good and a bad. In fact, bodies have been cut open in crude autopsies to try to find them! The Romans believed that the good spirit lived in their right-hand side and that their left was where the bad, chaotic spirit lived: hence, they believed, the reason why the left hand was less effective than the right. Indeed, the Latin word for 'left' has given us a word meaning dangerous and spooky: SINISTER. They also believed that if they walked into a house or room with their right foot first, then only the good spirit would enter. Hence the expression PUT YOUR BEST FOOT FORWARD. The importance of very carefully entering their right foot over the threshold has also given us a word based upon the Latin word for foot (*ped*) and meaning being overly precise: PEDANTIC. Other related words are the metal and plastic part of a bike or car that you push with the foot to control it: PEDAL; and a tradesmen who travels around on foot: PEDLAR.

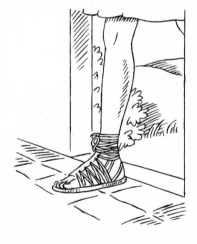

Amusingly, it is still a sailor's tradition always to step on to a ship right foot first – even if you are left-handed. This notion of the right side being good and lucky has also given us the phrase referring to someone being annoyed at having started the day with a bad omen: GETTING OUT OF THE BED ON THE WRONG SIDE; and similarly, for starting a conversation or relationship badly: GETTING OFF ON THE WRONG FOOT.

The Roman economy was heavily dependent upon slaves for both hard labour and domestic chores. Many slaves accepted their lot, among other reasons because the punishment for escaping was usually a horrible death. However, those who had just become slaves (by maybe being on the losing side in a war against Rome) were inclined to attempt escape if given half an opportunity. Aware of this, the Romans would often have the legs of these slaves loosely chained together. This reduced their effectiveness but at least prevented escape. The word for foot was *ped* and the word for 'putting on' was *im*, which has resulted in the word IMPEDE. Once they had become more trustworthy, the chains would be removed which would enable the slave to carry out their duties faster hence giving us the word meaning to release/accelerate something: EXPEDITE.

Another Roman belief was that when two people talked about a third person, angels would let the third person know by holding a burning torch to their ear. Hence the phrase HIS EARS ARE BURNING. If the discussion was positive it would be the right ear, if it was critical it was the left ear. Supposedly, if the person being talked about bit their own finger then the person talking would bite their tongue.

Well, I never knew that . . .
. . . euphoria always produces the right answers

Divination was an important part of Roman life, especially before any important event or activity. A popular practice was to examine the behaviour of birds or, on a messy day, even the entrails of birds and animals. There was a college of religious officials who released birds (*avis*) to 'see' (*spectare*) into the future. One of these priests would be called an *auspex* and the predictions that they made were called AUSPICES.

Hence anything that suggests a good future is still called AUSPICIOUS.

Auspices would always be taken before a major battle, although by law this could only be done by the commander-in-chief. This ensured that such an important influence on the army's morale could be interpreted in a positive way or be nudged in the right direction before it was announced to the soldiers. It also meant that if a junior officer played a crucial role in winning a victory, the commander-in-chief would be able to claim that it had been won UNDER THE AUSPICES of himself.

The emperors of Rome quickly learnt that leaving the answering of key questions to the temples gave the *auspex* a lot of power, and so they established a group of a dozen personally chosen men called *euphors* whom they could use for divining answers to politically critical questions such as whether Rome should go to war, or whether so-and-so was guilty of treason. Needless to say the *euphors* were well paid by the emperor and the answers would be what he was seeking. In fact they would make the emperor EUPHORIC.

Combining *auspex* with the Latin word for talk, *garrio* (from where we get 'garrulous') gives us another name for the seers: AUGURS. Their predictions were called AUGURIES, and from their high status and ability to make things official we get the word INAUGURATE. Hence also the phrase meaning that something is a good sign: IT AUGURS WELL FOR THE FUTURE.

When priests conducted an augury they would associate birds flying westwards, where the sun sets, with death and bad luck, and the east with good luck. In practice the west would be on their left-hand side and so again we have the Roman association of the left-hand or SINISTER side with evil or bad luck. Incidentally, the Roman word for right, combined with most people being right-handed, has given us a word meaning very physically adept and capable: DEXTROUS from *dexter* (right). Incidentally, both *sinister* and *dexter* are still used as terms in heraldry to describe the two sides of the shield.

The Latin word *ambi* means 'both'. So, for example, when both sides of an argument seem to have equal *value* the decision-maker may be AMBIVALENT. Equally, someone who is as capable with their left hand as with their right is said to be 'both-right-handed' or AMBIDEXTROUS. Incidentally, the French words for right and left – *droit* and *gauche* – give us more phrases. Someone who is very skilled or natural at something is called ADROIT. Someone who is unskilled, especially socially inept, is called GAUCHE.

The Romans put a great emphasis upon omens and if they perceived a negative omen they would often stop their planned course of action in fear of the consequences. The Latin word *ab*, meaning 'from' or 'away', was combined with *omen* to create a new word, *abomenable*, that was used to describe what terrors might await someone who ignores a negative omen and continues in the original direction or with their original plan – nowadays spelt ABOMINABLE.

Well, I never knew that . . .
. . . a new Pope always smokes

In ancient Rome the early soothsayers, called the Vaticanatores, erected a building on one of the hills, and the hill was named after them. Subsequently the hill has become the base of another religious organization, and the name of the hill has been applied to the city that has built up around this new entity: the VATICAN, named after the Mons Vaticanus or Vatican Hill. Incidentally, the Vatican is technically a city-state with its own money, government and guards. It is approximately a square mile in area with under one thousand inhabitants and famously includes the basilica of St Peter's, the papal palace and the Sistine Chapel.

When one pope dies, the next pope has to be chosen from a shortlist by a group of senior cardinals. These cardinals adjourn to the Sistine Chapel and start the discussions. A fire is lit and as long as the smoke remains dark it means that they have not yet made their decision. The first sign to the outside world that they have decided who will be the next pope is when they change the smoke to a much paler colour. This has given rise to a phrase used more widely to describe when a much-awaited decision has been made: SEEING THE WHITE SMOKE.

In the 4th century a cleric from Milan visited Rome and was surprised to see that the designated day for fasting in Rome was different from that which was observed in Milan. The cleric sought guidance from his cardinal – now known as St Ambrose. The cardinal's response is now well known in a shorter version: WHEN IN ROME, DO AS THE ROMANS DO. The full quote was: 'When in Milan, do as the Milanese do, when in Rome, do as the Romans do' – meaning, of course, follow the local customs so as to not to upset the local people.

Roman seers would often initially report bad omens and predict bad outcomes when first asked – and then suggest that donations to the temple might help things improve! The Latin word *monstro*, meaning 'to show', was used to describe these grim prospects and over time became associated with scary outcomes and situations even without a seer being involved. Through association with dreams, the word evolved to describe the embodiment of fear and danger in scary imaginary animals: MONSTROUS and MONSTERS. Yet another derivative of *monstro* gives us the word for showing someone that something is not scary by removing (de-) the imagined monster: DEMONSTRATE.

The idea of shape-changing monsters becoming human and then becoming monsters again in nightmares led the Roman poet Ovid to use the Greek word *morphe* (meaning 'shape') as the name for a god of dreams: MORPHEUS. Many centuries later this god was used to name a drug designed to put patients into a dreamy state to reduce pain: MORPHINE. Also, when insects change their shape (*meta* in Latin) in turning, for example, from caterpillars to butterflies, we use the word METAMORPHOSIS.

The Romans observed that there was an increase in fatal feverish illness during the summer months. At the same time the marshes around Rome would also begin to smell. They therefore assumed that the illness was caused by the air itself and called the illness 'bad air' – or, as we know it, MALARIA. Of course we now know that the disease was in fact caused by the mosquitoes that lived in the swamp and bred, hence increasing their numbers, at that time of year.

Incidentally, in Renaissance France it was thought that fresh 'good' air was very important for health, and so we get the expression for someone who looks healthy and bright: 'of good air' or, in French, DEBONAIR.   **WINKT!**

7

Roman Law and Politics

Odd as it sounds, modern law
students still study Roman law – so
what was it all about and what does
it have to do with us?

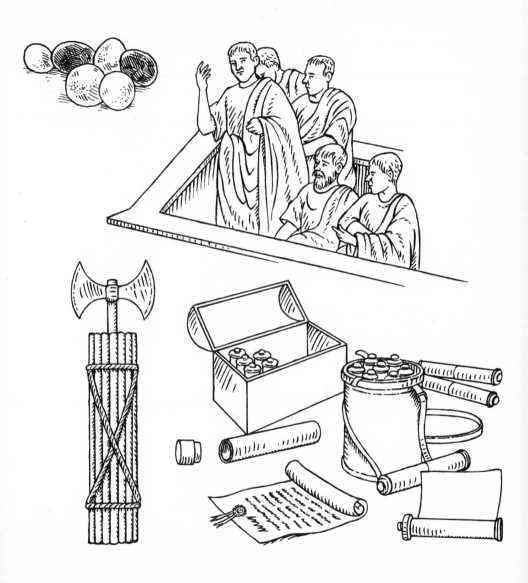

Well, I never knew that . . .
. . . Cicero's ladle is still with us

The Latin word for elder is *senior,* which we use in the same form in phrases such as SENIOR CITIZEN, etc. Many countries have evolved a form of this word that conveys respect for such a person, and in some cases is also a formal title for an individual empowered by the king. Hence in England we have SIR; in Spain, SEÑOR; in France, MONSIEUR; in Italy, SIGNOR.

In ancient Rome, to vote for a candidate involved placing a white (or sometimes red) ball or pebble into a container, or a black ball to vote against a candidate: hence the phrase TO BLACKBALL SOMEONE, meaning to exclude them.

The Roman statesman Cicero derided someone who was trying to make a big issue about something that really did not matter by saying that he had 'made waves in a ladle'. The phrase stuck and evolved over time, via glasses and wash basins, to the phrase that we know today: A STORM IN A TEACUP.

Well, I never knew that . . .
. . . a dazzling politician might not be as honest as he looks

Roman politicians were very image-conscious (nothing new there then!) and when seeking votes for election they would have white chalk rubbed into their already white togas to make them appear shining white – attracting attention and conveying purity and honesty to those who saw them. These extra white clothes were named *candidus*, meaning 'glowing white'. The individuals were then named after these clothes: CANDIDATES. Two shorter evolutions of the word still convey the sense of honesty and openness: CANDOUR and CANDID.

As they walked around Rome trying to win support, the candidates would have special assistants by their side to whisper the names and roles of important people whom they met. Given that *clator* was Latin for 'caller' and *nomen* was Latin for 'name', these men became known by a term that we still use to describe the correct naming of people and things: NOMENCLATURE.

On one occasion when several Roman senators failed to attend an important Senate meeting, slaves were sent out across the city with rope soaked in dye to wrap around and mark the senators not present in an effort to embarrass them. Hence the phrase for being reluctantly coerced into doing something: BEING ROPED IN.

The senior magistrates in Rome were very powerful people. They could in theory deliver a death sentence on the spot as they walked around the city; they were attended by men called *lictors* who carried symbolic bundles of sticks with which people could be beaten, and a double-headed axe with which people could be beheaded. This symbol can often be seen in legal documents. The bundle – *fasces* in Latin – was tied together with a red cord and was designed to remind everyone of the power, ultimately over people's lives, that these magistrates had. Two thousand years later this concept was applied again in Italy by a new political party trying to stamp out the rising popularity of the socialists in the lead-up to the First World War. Hence the name of the party: the FASCISTS. Eventually, in 1922, the King of Italy was forced to appoint the leader of these rebels as Prime Minister; in 1925 he took over from the King as a dictator, basing his model of power on that of ancient Rome. He even adopted the symbol of the *fasces* as his party's logo. His name was BENITO MUSSOLINI.

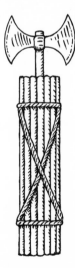

Incidentally, the tradition of using red cords to tie the lictors' equipment together continues to this day with red ribbon still being used by lawyers to wrap up sets of legal documents. In fact this association with complex, difficult to understand documents has become associated with bureaucracy in general and gives us the term RED TAPE.

As we have seen, the consuls were the most powerful men of all. Either consul could stop any debate taking place in the Senate by simply saying 'I forbid it', from which we get a Latin word used a great deal in negotiation and meaning literally 'I forbid': VETO.

The Roman Senate was always a hotbed of politics and intrigue where secret deals would be done behind the scenes. However, ultimately senators had to vote by standing up in the Senate building. This was where they had to let everyone know who and what they supported. This gives us two phrases: STAND UP AND BE COUNTED and literally LET EVERYONE KNOW WHERE YOU STAND.

Well, I never knew that . . .
. . . screens and scrolls gave us treasurers and treatises

Rome was one of the first nations to write down all of its laws in detail. This was done on scrolls of either papyrus or parchment (made from animal skins).

In the Roman Empire important scrolls would often have a summary and index glued on to the very top of a document as the first item. The Greek word for glue was *kolla*, and the word for 'first' was *prot*. The summary would often be read out at the start of meetings, and so the name of this front page came to be used to describe the purpose of the meeting. Over time this section included not just the summary but also the outline of how a discussion or treaty negotiation would be conducted. Thus the word is now used to clarify how things should be done: PROTOCOL.

Most Roman writing was done on parchment or vellum scrolls which were then rolled up and stored in boxes or leather scroll-cases. Large documents would be split among several scrolls. Using the Latin word for 'to roll', *volvare*, we get the term for each roll, now used for each part of a work published in more than one book or series: VOLUME 1,

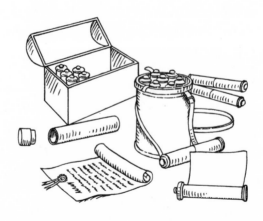

VOLUME 2, etc. The word was then used to describe the number of scrolls that a box could contain. Different-sized boxes were then referred to by their capacity to hold a certain number of scrolls, and so the word evolved into meaning the capacity of each box. Hence our second modern meaning of the word VOLUME. As a larger box of scrolls would take more reading out to convey the contents than a smaller box, the word 'volume' became associated with the amount of talking and hence loudness, and then to loudness in general. Hence we have another meaning related to loudness: VOLUME (of sound).

Incidentally, using the prefix *con-*, which means together, we get a term for the complications of trying to reconcile two separate scrolls that relate to each other but in a way that is difficult to understand: CONVOLUTED. Rolling two scrolls together into the same storage tube because they do fit together gives us a word meaning bringing two things together: INVOLVE. Rolling something out and then rolling it back up to put away gives us the word which we tend to use in the sense of continuous rolling: REVOLVE.

Rolling a scroll over is equivalent to turning it over. The Latin word *volta*, meaning to turn, gives us an expression for when we completely change our outlook (i.e. as if literally turning our head in the opposite direction) and conclusions on a subject: VOLTE-FACE.

Cancelli is the Latin word for 'screen'. Such a lattice screen was used to separate lawyers from other people in Roman courts of law. A clerk sat at the *cancelli* to enable controlled communication between the public and the inner workings of the court. The title of this clerk was taken from the name of the screen. Over a thousand years later the same title was reused by Edward the Confessor to describe the noble responsible for overseeing the spiritual aspects of the King's rule and communicating on his behalf with the Church in Rome. Over time this powerful noble increasingly adopted additional responsibilities, including the creation of legal documents and then the use of the great seal to authorize documents in the King's name. The title allotted to this noble (derived from *cancelli*) was CHANCELLOR.

A similar screen to the *cancelli* in law courts was used to split the main part of a church from the altar and choir area. Hence this part of the church became known as the CHANCEL. The screen retained the mystery and ceremony of the service and hid the detail from the common people who were considered far too unsophisticated to appreciate it or show it sufficient respect. From the practice of priests carrying a cross on top of a rod around a church the word rod or 'rood' came to be associated with elevated crosses. As the new screens in churches always had a cross at the top they were called ROOD SCREENS.

The role of the chancellor soon also covered responsibility for the finances of the King and country. The inflow and outflow of money, especially taxes and other payments due from nobles, were monitored using a very large chequered cloth (similar to a chess/chequers board). Hence the title became CHANCELLOR OF THE EXCHEQUER. The room and subsequently the government department was also known as the Exchequer.

During the medieval period when the role was expanding, Henry II made his closest friend both Chancellor *and* Archbishop of Canterbury, assuming that he would have a loyal and trusted person in this vital role. However, his friend adopted a confrontational style and resolutely upheld the independence of the Church and its finances. Ultimately this led to the King making an uncontrolled outburst about how such a disloyal man should not be tolerated. Taking the King at his word, four knights went off and killed him. The archbishop's name was THOMAS À BECKET.

In Britain we have the Queen as head of state and a Prime Minister who in theory at least is subordinate to her. When the new German Empire was created in 1871, Bismarck became the leader of the government and adopted the title of Chancellor, at the time equivalent to the British Prime Minister. However, since the First World War there has not been a Kaiser (German king), and so the Chancellor is now the most senior figure in the German State.

Incidentally it is believed that the 'c' of Caesar was pronounced as we would say a 'k' and so the title Kaiser is in fact a pretty good emulation of the two-thousand-year-old Roman title of Caesar.

Incidentally, the section of the English law courts that looks after business-related matters (bankruptcy, probate, shares, etc.) is called the Chancery (a shortened form of Chancellery) and is headed by the Lord Chancellor – a completely different role from the Chancellor of the Exchequer, although both names are ultimately derived from the same Roman clerk. The road in London where the Chancellery used to be located is still called CHANCERY LANE! Commercial and probate cases are very complex, so they tend to last a long time and can be exhausting for all parties. Hence the term used in boxing where one boxer tries to drag out a fight by holding the other boxer's head down against the rules: IN CHANCERY.

Well, I never knew that . . .
. . . you had to have balls to stand up in court!

Rome suffered from robbers just as any modern city of its size would. These thugs would often operate in gangs and beset their victims by grabbing their clothes. Now, cloaks were popular in Rome because they could be left open in the heat and pulled close during the much cooler nights. They also had the advantage that if a robber grabbed your cloak you could simply slip it over your head and run away, leaving him just with the cloak. Using the word '*ex*' meaning out and '*cape*' for cloak we get the word ESCAPE.

The Romans put great emphasis upon their legal system, especially the use of witnesses. The use of such third parties who were separate from the two protagonists gave rise to the word for such witnesses – *testis*, developed from an older word that had meant 'third'. The legal use of this word has resulted in several words still used today: the process of giving evidence, to TESTIFY; the content of a statement, a TESTAMENT; and to state something vehemently, ATTEST. The idea of a man acting in this way led to the word being associated with honour and eventually to a man's self-worth, virility and manliness. Hence the word for a part of a man's body closely associated with his virility: TESTICLE.

In ancient Rome, when a debtor could not pay the person to whom he owed money, a court of law could decide that he become that person's slave until the debt was paid. They were known by a word that we now use very differently. Using the Latin *ad* (to) and *dicere* (say) we get the term that describes someone who is told (or compelled through habit) to do things that they don't really want to do as if a slave: ADDICT. So people really can be 'slaves' to their addiction!   **WINKT!**

8

Latin, Rome and English

The English language can be
mystifyingly complicated and
intoxicatingly rich – and a lot of it
comes from Rome!

Well, I never knew that . . .
. . . the Romans chucked the Latins out but kept their language!

Before Romulus founded Rome, in 753 BC, the area was inhabited by a pretty lacklustre tribe of people called the Latini. The area was therefore called Latinum, and when the Romans established themselves they adopted the existing local language – hence LATIN. But how important has Latin been to the English language?

Well, the English language is the richest and most subtle language in the world, with words coming from many different languages and sources. As an example, we get a term from the French word *nuer*, originally meaning the *shadow* under a cloud but used eventually to mean the subtle hints of shade implied through the careful use of words: NUANCE. Equally, we could say that something has

THE SHADES of something else. Indeed, it is the rich background that lies behind the language that offers English-language speakers such a range of nuances in what they say.

The original 'Old English' derived from Germanic and Saxon sources nowadays makes up no more than 25 per cent of the modern English language. The French language that arrived with William the Conqueror and his 10,000 Norman followers took over as the language of rule within England, despite the fact that the invaders were massively outnumbered by more than 2,000,000 Anglo-Saxons. Nevertheless, the Normans did enforce their language, to the extent that 27 per cent of our modern language is directly related to this form of old French. Greek constitutes another 8 per cent of our language, but the biggest single source of words, at over 28 per cent, is Latin. This arrived through several routes, including the Roman Empire, the Catholic Church, and many indirect routes, for example via Spanish.

Let's explore some examples.

Well, I never knew that . . .

. . . creamy puddings have a lot in common with sand dunes

De- is often used in Latin to mean 'the opposite'. So the opposite of positively announcing someone is to DENOUNCE them. *Sperare* is the Latin word for hope. Without it you 'despare' or DESPAIR, and perhaps become DE-SPERATE. If you want to remove something that has already been attached you DETACH it (i.e. de-attach).

Tegere (and thence *tect*) is Latin for 'to cover'. Hence, to uncover something is to DE-TECT it. Someone who specializes in doing this is a DETECTIVE. *Via* is Latin for road, also meaning the main way. If you choose an alternative route, you DE-VIATE. The opposite of *filling* something (*plere* = to fill) is to DEPLETE it. As a slave or *servant* you are expected to *serve* others without pay. If you do serve others when you do not have to then you merit an award: in other words, you DE-SERVE something in return. The opposite of following a *river* to the sea is to track it back to its source: DERIVE. *Sere* is Latin meaning 'to bind'. If an area of land is so barren that there is nothing there to bind farmers or anyone else to the land, it is called a DESERT. And if a soldier is unhappy about being bound to the rules of any of the armed services, he may choose to become a DESERTER.

Des- usually means 'away' or 'separately'. For example, a line in a song (*cantus* in Latin) that is sung separately from everyone else is a DESCANT. And last but not least, when we are served with the last course of a meal before we leave and separate from the friends we have bonded (*sere*) with all evening, we partake of a des-sert or DESSERT. Hence the connection (i.e. they are *bound* together by the word *sere*) between désert, desért and dessert and why only dessert has a double 's'!

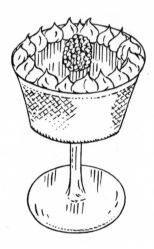

Crastinus is Latin for tomorrow. This word was used as part of a phrase meaning to defer a decision or action until tomorrow, using the Latin word *pro*, meaning 'for', as in leaving something 'for tomorrow': thus we get PROCRASTINATE.

Caput is Latin for head. So when the Romans *beheaded* wrongdoers the people were DECAPITATED. A hat that goes on the *head* is called a CAP and when a maximum limit is put on the top of something it is said to be CAPPED. When a ship sinks it sometimes turns over with its '*head*' going underwater. Such ships are said to have CAPSIZED. The *head* of a unit of soldiers is called a CAPTAIN. Also, second sons of noblemen who were not going to inherit a fortune would often have to give their services for free to the army in the hope that they would rise through the ranks and capture a fortune through warfare. These aspirational young officers were called *small captains* or *capdets* – what we know as CADETS.

In Latin, *posterior* means 'behind' and *pre* means 'in front'. In Rome, if an idea was suggested that was clearly the result of muddled thinking, the Romans would say that the idea was both 'in front' and 'behind': PREPOSTEROUS.

Com had the meaning of 'together' or 'shared'. Hence when two things come together we get a word using this prefix with *binary* (meaning two): COMBINE. When things are pressed (*pact* in Latin) together they are COMPACTED, or even COMPRESSED. The name for a strongly defended position comes from the

Latin (and French) word for strong: FORT. Related to this, if you share your own strength with someone else who needs it you COMFORT them. *Com* plus *panis* (bread) gives us the word for close friends who share their bread with each other: COMPANIONS. *Panis*, incidentally, also gives us the word for the bags that were slung over donkeys' backs to carry bread around a town: PANNIERS. In the 17th century merchants in London began to congregate together in the London coffee-houses, where they clubbed together to fund exciting trading ventures. These groupings of friends became known as COMPANIES. Interestingly, in English law these companies are treated in most respects as persons, and so using the Latin word for body, *corpus*, they are also called CORPORATIONS.

Im means 'not' or 'the opposite', hence IMPOSSIBLE, IMBALANCE, IMMORAL. When two things collide as opposed to being pressed together they IMPACT.

Pare means 'equal', from where we get the word for two things that are equal: A PAIR. A score in sport (e.g. golf) that a good player should be able to equal is PAR, and people who are your equals are PEERS. Incidentally, when the Normans invaded Britain in 1066 they only considered other Norman knights as equals and hence we have PEERS OF THE REALM. When you bring two things together to see if they are equal you COMPARE THEM.

Well, I never knew that . . .
. . . waves of well-being can make you feel fabulous

Pose is Latin and Greek for place. Hence a specific place is a POSITION. To put parts of a model's body in specific places is TO POSE the model. To bring things together (*com*) into the same place is to COMPOSE. Using the prefix *de-*, meaning away, we get the term for money that is placed 'away' and to some extent out of reach for a specific purpose: DEPOSIT. Equally, a ruler who is 'placed away' from his previous role is DEPOSED.

The word 'fable' comes from the Latin word *fari*, meaning 'to speak'. If something appears to be so good that it is as if it were from a great story or fable about faraway magical kingdoms, it is described as FABULOUS.

The old word for reckoning was *putare*. Hence the process of bringing several numbers together to be 'reckoned' is *computare*, or to COMPUTE. A machine that does this is a COMPUTER.

Unda was Latin for a surging wave, and so a series of good harvests that created a 'wave' of good feeling from the surplus of food was said to be ABUNDANT.

The Latin word for a lathe is *tornos*, meaning 'to turn'. This also gives us the profession of someone who does this work (and the associated surname): TURNER. Sometimes a cord needs to be tightened around an arm either to stop severe bleeding or to make the veins stand out. This used to be achieved by inserting a stick and *twisting* it to gradually tighten the cord. This is called a TOURNIQUET. Before jousting had been invented, when medieval knights used to meet to show off their fighting skills they would compete in large mêlées which required a lot of twisting and turning to prevent being attacked from behind. Such competitions were called TOURNAMENTS, often shortened to TOURNEYS. Expeditions often have a particular destination in mind but include several other sites en route. When the travellers reach the ultimate destination they will then turn around and RETURN to the start point. Such expeditions are called TOURS.

The Latin word *genu* meant 'bend'. Hence we get the term for bending in a bowing motion to show respect to a superior: GENUFLECT. The same root also gives us the term for the part of the leg that bends: KNEE, as well as the suffix added to words that describe how many bends or corners there are in a geometric shape: *-gon* as in POLYGON, HEXAGON, etc. Some people also believe that the Romans' habit of genuflecting only to people whom you fully accept as socially superior gives us the word GENUINE. However, others believe it carries the sense of pure-bred via the word *genus* meaning 'born'.

The Romans used the word *signum* to mean a mark or to point something out. By the Middle Ages the Latin-speaking Church used the word to describe how a priest moved his hand in the shape of a cross when making a blessing, i.e. to make a SIGN OF THE CROSS. This led to the word being used more widely. For example, a picture put up outside an inn would be called an INN SIGN. A ring that left a specific mark in wax was called a SIGNET RING. Symbols that showed that an individual was part of a larger group were called INSIGNIA. When a message was sent by using flags or other visual

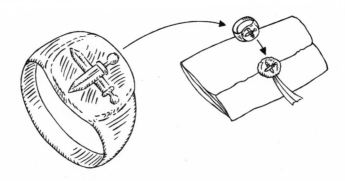

methods it was called SIGNALLING. Before long, flags that indicated that a senior officer or leader was present were known as ENSIGNS. In the army and navy, the person responsible for holding such a flag was also called an ENSIGN. A very important sign would be SIGNIFICANT, and indeed a Roman soldier who carried (*fero* = 'carry') was called a SIGNIFER. Eventually, the very personal sign of an individual who wrote their own name was called a SIGNATURE.

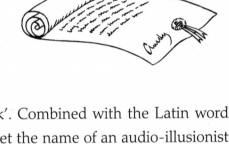

Loqui is Latin for 'to speak'. Combined with the Latin word for stomach – *vente* – we get the name of an audio-illusionist act who appears to speak from his tummy: VENTRILOQUIST. Someone who speaks a great deal is LOQUACIOUS. Someone who speaks very elegantly is said to be ELOQUENT. And someone who pronounces their words very clearly is said to have good ELOCUTION. A common way that people use words together (Latin *co-*) is COLLOQUIAL. **WINKT!**

9

Everyday Life in Rome

So what did these Romans do when
they weren't out on the campaign
trail or killing Christians in the
amphitheatre? Well, their home life
was surprisingly mundane (and that's
a word that comes from Latin . . .)

Well, I never knew that . . .
. . . writing in Rome was a matter of style

Papyrus, invented by the Egyptians, was still relatively rare in the days of Rome, and so for many people writing was done simply by scratching basic words onto thin sheets of lead made especially for the purpose, or onto wax tablets that were kept inside wooden boxes so that the wax could be melted down and reused. In both cases a sharp point was needed to makes the scratches, and this was provided by specially made metal 'pins' called *styli*. Polite society considered neat letters to be important and indicative of a person's own character and personality, and so today we have the words derived from these items: STYLE and STYLISH. Closer to the original  meaning is our term for the metal end of a fountain pen that writes with ink: STYLUS. The same word, incidentally, again referring to the pen or pin, was used to describe the fine needle that was used to play vinyl records: STYLUS.

The difficulty of scratching with these items meant that block capital letters, using straight lines, were easiest to write, and in fact the idea of lower-case letters did not emerge until well after the end of the western Roman Empire.

Before the idea of cellulose paper had arrived in Europe from China, the Romans would sometimes peel bark away from certain trees to reveal the smooth inner bark. This could then be used for writing upon. Using the Latin word for 'to peel', *liber*, we get the French word for book, *livre*, and the English word for a place where books are stored, LIBRARY. Interestingly, the same source also gives us the word for unfair *written* defamation of someone's character: LIBEL. The idea of 'peeling' something off also gives us the word for freeing something or someone, LIBERATE, and for liquid that is poured off from a jug, LIBATION.

Like the Greeks, the Romans loved their theatre and in fact created a new form that involved a single actor performing on stage. He would tell a story to music through mime and wear a series of different, brightly coloured masks as he played each different character. The stories were often beyond belief and were set in many exciting and far-off parts of the Empire. The actor would often develop humorous interaction with the audience, especially in some of the more unbelievable elements of the story. By combining the word 'mime' with the word for 'many' (characters), *pan*, we get a term that we still use today for a fantastic humorous stage show with music: PANTOMIME.

One particular metal was very important to Mediterranean civilizations, used both in alloys in making weapons and in pure form for coinage and jewellery. The Romans called it *aes*, and the biggest source that they found was on the island of Cyprus, which they invaded in 58 BC to get control of the ore. They called this ore *aes cyprium*. However, as 'u' and 'y' were the same letter in the Roman alphabet, it was commonly called *aes cuprium* or just *cuprium* for short. From this we get both the anglicized version of the name: COPPER and the chemical symbol Cu.

The Romans saw Rome as the very heart of the world and regarded the sea around Rome as the middle of the world.

Hence, from the words *medius* (middle) and *terra* (earth) we get the name MEDITERRANEAN.

In ancient Rome many slaves had holes bored into their earlobes to show that they were slaves. The same mechanism was used in medieval times on cattle and other livestock, with various shaped holes or cuts showing who had bought which animals. At the end of trading, the new owners would then return and collect the animals they had previously EARMARKED.

Well, I never knew that . . .
. . . too much conviviality might lead to a bastard

In Turkey the Romans came across a goddess-based religion whose ceremonies involved priestesses dancing themselves into a frenzy and then ripping their clothes and cutting themselves with knives. The Roman word for temple was *fanum,* and so they called these priestesses FANATICS. Eventually the word came to be used to describe someone with an unusually intense interest in a particular topic or person, and subsequently an adapted version has become commonplace: FAN.

Only priests and a chosen few were allowed to see the inner workings of temples and key ceremonies; the others, who were kept outside (*pro* is Latin for outside) were called PROFANE.

The Romans observed that dogs and some people would tend to act unusually at the time of a full moon. This led to a word that is used to this day to describe unpredictable behaviour,

from *luna* (moon): LUNATIC. A related expression comes from the belief that if one's head was struck by moonlight while sleeping one could be driven mad: MOONSTRUCK.

The Latin for packsaddle is *bastum*. From the idea of a barmaid's night of passion with a traveller staying at an inn and the birth of a child nine months later comes our word BASTARD.

The Latin word for 'to give birth' is *parere*. From this comes our English word PARENT. The Romans combined this word with their word for 'life' – *vivus* – to name a snake that they thought gave birth to live young: *vivus-parere* or VIPER. A word that uses the same root (*vivus*) to convey the meaning 'full of life' is VIVACIOUS; another, which conveys the idea of adding to the enjoyment for life, is CONVIVIAL.

Well, I never knew that . . .
. . . plumbers and pencils lead back to the same place

Water pipes used to be made of lead, and the Latin for lead is *plumbus*. This is why, when something goes wrong with the water pipes in your house, you call a PLUMBER to deal with the PLUMBING. Eventually it was found that using lead pipes to transport drinking water over many years resulted in lead poisoning, and building regulations were changed to stop the use of lead piping and replace it initially with copper, and more recently with plastic, which is cheaper.

If you want an absolute vertical line you use a thread with a lead weight on the end: a PLUMB LINE. If you have a perfectly vertical line, it is said to be PLUMB STRAIGHT. The small lead weight itself was called a 'plombet', and because it went straight down, it gave us the word for the action of falling (by implication very fast) straight downwards: PLUMMET. Also, someone who is very confident and fashionable and who dresses and stands in a way that grabs attention, perhaps like the impact of a totally perpendicular column, is said to have APLOMB. And of course, if you try something out with an audience and it fails dismally, it WENT DOWN LIKE A LEAD BALLOON!

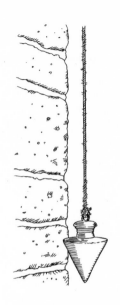

In the days of galleons, lead weights on the end of a rope would be thrown out ahead of a ship and the depth of water assessed by how far down the rope went. This gives us the term PLUMBING THE DEPTHS. This was considered an easy task, and so we get the term A PLUMB (often spelled PLUM) JOB.

The Greek word for 'written' or 'drawn' was *graphos*; hence the term for numbers presented in picture form, GRAPHS, and for anything presented in a way that is easy to 'picture' in your mind, GRAPHIC. Also, the name of the dark substance in pencils that can be used to draw is GRAPHITE.

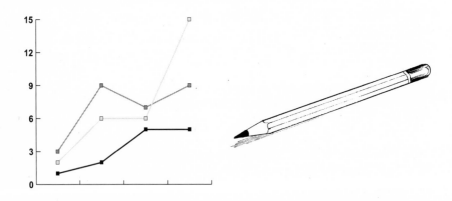

Alchemists thought that the almost pure form of carbon now known as graphite was in fact mainly lead, and so they called it *plumbago*. Hence the incorrect name given to the graphite within pencils: LEAD (originally referred to as 'blacklead'). The graphite in pencils is in fact a form of carbon with no lead in it at all.

When the ruins of Pompeii were being uncovered and explored in the mid-1850s, many words and phrases were found scratched on the walls of buildings. These were collectively named after the Italian word meaning 'I have scratched' (*graffito*), from which we get the modern word GRAFFITI.

The Colosseum was a massive architectural achievement that was built specifically to house gladiatorial games. Its design incorporated many arches (*fornix* in Latin), which both

reduced the total weight of the structure and gave it a very striking appearance. Tens of thousands of men and rather fewer women attended the gladiatorial games, and prostitutes found that after the games the testosterone-charged men would prove to be willing customers, often there and then in the shadows of the arches. Hence we get the word FORNICATION. This is also why various arch-shaped structures in the human body are called the *fornix*.

Well, I never knew that . . .
. . . a pungent smell goes right through you

The Roman word for day – *dies* – derives in turn from an even older Indo-European word used to describe the very important god of the sky. This also gives us the word used to describe a god: DEITY.

In ancient Rome, various writers claimed to be able to write summaries of plays in very small handwriting on pieces of paper such that they could be folded within the shell of a walnut. This skill was greatly admired by people such as Pliny the Elder, and gave us a phrase still used today that implies a very concise summary: IN A NUTSHELL.

Pungere was Latin meaning 'to strike' or 'to pierce'. From this we get the word for a blow with a fist – PUNCH – and also for the mechanical device that makes holes: a HOLE PUNCH. Also, a piercing smell is PUNGENT, and the effect of a piercing blow is a PUNCTURE. From the same source come the word for grabbing flesh prior to piercing it – PINCHING – and the name for scissors that leave a jagged edge as if the fabric had been roughly pierced: PINKING SHEARS.

The Latin word *ducere* meaning 'to lead' gives us the word for a channel or tube that leads or directs air or water to its destination: DUCT – and, in particular, a channel that leads water (*aqua*) towards a city even over hills and valleys: AQUEDUCT; also the word for the process of reasoning from a series of facts or clues to lead back to an original event: DEDUCE (*de-* meaning opposite).

Oriens was Latin for rising. Hence the Romans called the land where the sun rises (i.e. in the east) the Orient. By checking where the sun rises it is also possible to clarify in which direction you need to go; hence we call this ORIENTATION.

Desilire is Latin for 'jumping down', which was the basis of the name *desulores*, given to Roman circus acts where riders would jump onto horses, jump between them and perform various daring acts while mounted on them. From the idea of jumping around from one mount to another we get a word nowadays used to describe something disconnected or directionless: DESULTORY.

In Rome, *paganus* meant 'country dweller'. As the Roman Empire spread and had to conquer less civilized societies with no major towns, whose people had their own gods, these people became known as PAGANS. When the barbarian invasions forced the Romans to withdraw from Britain and north-west Europe, the small communities that had built up around the Roman *villas* would often remain a focal point for settlements, giving us the term VILLAGES. During the early Middle Ages the peasants who lived near the villa (or, later, the village) were called, non-judgementally, VILLANS (i.e. people of the village). However, *villes* came to be used as a derogatory term by the invading Norman lords, who would typically live in castles for protection and not trust the Anglo-Saxons who lived in the villages. So when the Black Death killed about 30 per cent of the UK population and the result-ing manpower shortage led to the peasants demanding more pay, then revolting when they did not get it, a similar term as applied to these rebellious Saxon peasants, but this time with definitely negative connotations: VILLAINS.

The Romans invented a way of combining small stones called *camentum* with volcanic ash and lime from near the town of Pozzuoli. This was used as an early form of concrete. Over time the ash and lime mix without the stones began to be used in construction and ironically was named after the stones themselves: CEMENT. Nowadays there are two common types of cement. One is named after the Roman mines: POZZOLANA CEMENT. The other was developed in the early 19th century by a British man who patented a mixture of clay and limestone and called it after the natural stone that it looked like when it set hard: PORTLAND CEMENT, after Portland stone – at the time a very popular stone for large buildings, especially in London and other large cities. Incidentally, 75 years before Portland cement was patented, an earlier version had been created that would set under water. This was needed to build the Eddystone Lighthouse. This was seen as such a success that it made the inventor and designer, John Smeaton, very famous; indeed, so renowned was his lighthouse that when it was replaced the original lighthouse was re-erected on Plymouth Hoe, where it can still be visited today. It is known as SMEATON'S TOWER.

Well, I never knew that . . .
. . . a dog and its house come from the same place

In ancient Rome there was a word for the main fireplace of a house. Through the ages such fireplaces have provided the *centre* for the home around which family members will often gather together, especially on cold evenings. This idea of bringing people's attention *together* then adopted the original Latin word for fireplace. During the Renaissance scientists used the same word to describe the point at which a

magnifying glass could create a fire by *concentrating* the sun's rays on a piece of paper and heating it to the crucial temperature. The Latin word originally meaning fireplace is  FOCUS, and the subsequent phrase is FOCAL POINT. This association with fire led to the French word *feu* and the Spanish word *fuego*, both meaning 'fire'. Combined with the suffix *aille* (in this case meaning 'material') we have a word meaning material for a fire: *feu-aille* or FUEL.

Turbe was the Latin word for 'shaking'. Hence we get the word for when something has been shaken up: DISTURBED. When someone's happiness has been shaken up, they are PERTURBED. When the air has been shaken up by the weather, we experience TURBULENCE. The idea of turbulence associated with a whirlwind then formed the basis of a new type of engine that created a controlled whirlwind: a TURBINE. Subsequently a device was developed that used a turbine in the exhaust pipe of an engine to create power to force more air into the engine and hence increase its power – giving us a TURBO-CHARGED engine. Incidentally, where air is forced into an engine by a separately powered device instead of a turbo charger it is called SUPER-CHARGED.

Dogs were popular pets in ancient Rome. In fact, the Roman word for dog – *canis* – gives us the word for anything that is dog-like, such as sharp incisor teeth, CANINE TEETH. Romans used dogs mainly for guard duties, and hence, from the Latin phrase *cave canum* (*cave* meaning 'beware'), we get

the well-known sign still used to deter intruders and warn postmen: BEWARE OF THE DOG. Even the word we use for a dog's shelter came originally from the Latin *canile*: KENNEL.

The wives of senior Roman army officers would often have specially bred small dogs for company that they could easily carry around themselves in their sedan chairs. These were called by a term often used nowadays to describe someone who is totally under the control of someone else as if they are 'owned': LAP DOGS.   **WINKT!**

10
Roman Food

The Romans didn't have pasta or tomatoes – so what did they eat, and why were their salads always salty?

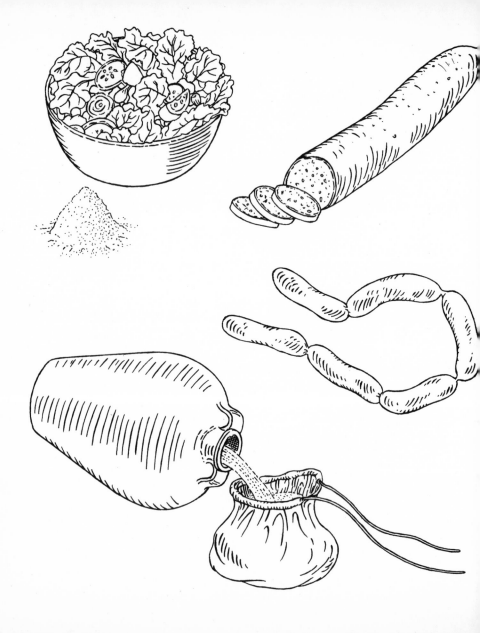

Menu
À la
Carte

Well, I never knew that . . .
. . . good Roman legionaries really were
worth their salt

Incredible as it may seem, two of the things we most strongly associate with Italian food did not exist in ancient Rome. In fact it was not until around AD 750 that the predecessors to the Aztecs in South America successfully cultivated the Xiotamtl plant, and then it was another 800 years before Spanish explorers brought it back to Europe. Even then it was shunned for many years because of concerns that it might be poisonous. This fear was partly because it comes from the same family of plants as deadly nightshade, and the doubt persisted even in Britain until the 19th century. Now we have no such suspicion of the plant's fruit, which we know as TOMATOES.

As for pasta, this was invented in China before the Roman Empire but was only eaten in Europe after the intrepid explorer Marco Polo brought the idea back to Italy in the 13th century. Of course, the Chinese know it as NOODLES.

Incidentally, the Romans did not have a particular exotic fruit either, even though it often incorrectly appears in Hollywood reconstructions of ancient Roman feasts! The name comes simply from the outer similarity to a pine cone and the resemblance of the fleshy inside to a juicy apple: PINEAPPLE. This fruit would not appear in Europe until it was brought back from South America in the 16th century.

The Latin word *mare* for the 'sea' crops up in a lot of our words that are connected with the sea, including, for example, soldiers trained to fight at sea, MARINES, and also the word for soaking meat or other food in a salty liquid to add flavour, MARINADE – as well as, of course, the word that describes anything to do with the sea: MARITIME.

Latin has given us many words from the Latin word *dormire*, meaning to sleep. For example, the room where people sleep together is a DORMITORY. Animals, or even computers, that are currently 'asleep' are DORMANT. A small rodent famous for sleeping is a DORMOUSE – which is why of course it is a single 'o' and not a double 'o' as in 'door'. The Latin is also clearly the source of the French word to sleep – *dormir*.

The Roman lower classes were called plebeians, from which we get the derogatory insult PLEB. Roman plebeians ate a great deal of bread, while the rich enjoyed much more luxurious food, with all the types of meat that we are used to plus delicacies such as fattened dormice that would be kept in specially made clay pots!

At the time of the Roman Empire, few spices had worked their way westwards from India and the Far East, and chilli peppers from South and Central America had not yet been  discovered by Europeans. So the Romans became dependent upon one type of food to enhance the flavour – SALT. Because Italy is a long, thin peninsula surrounded by sea, everyone had easy access to it, and it had the added benefit of preserving foods as well as accentuating flavours.

A bit like burgers in the modern American army, which are so popular that it is deemed important to set up McDonald's restaurants early on in new US military bases, salt was very important for Roman soldiers. This was partly through preference, but also because soldiers who marched all day in the Mediterranean heat needed to replace the salt lost through perspiration. In fact, this was such an inherent part of a soldier's life that the ingenious Romans decided to pay their soldiers partially in salt. Hence our word SALARY, from the Latin *sale*, salt. This had the added benefit that there was less need to have so many cartloads of silver following the army around in enemy territory!

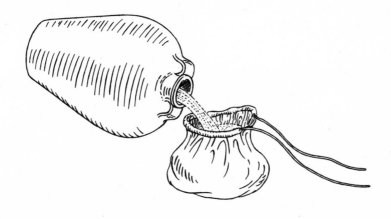

If a Roman soldier failed to perform his duties correctly he would have his pay reduced or cut altogether for a period of time, as he was NOT WORTH HIS SALT! Of course, if a soldier fell asleep on guard duty or was guilty of anything equally serious, the punishment was a great deal harsher. If the colleagues in their unit were put at risk by his dereliction, the individual would be stripped naked and forced to run along between two lines of soldiers who would strike him on the head and shoulders with clubs or wooden sticks. If the whole unit was put at risk, the sentence could be as severe as stoning to death. In contrast, a soldier consistently doing more than his duty and admired by his colleagues would be called THE SALT OF THE EARTH.

Incidentally, the process of salting meat to enable it to be stored for future use has given us a phrase often used for saving money 'for a rainy day': SALTING AWAY. And acknowledging the importance of being loyal to your employer who pays your salary is the source of the phrase BEING TRUE TO ONE'S SALT.

Because the Romans considered salt to be so valuable, both as payment and for purifying and preserving, spilling salt was therefore very unlucky and an ill omen. When salt was spilled, whoever caused the accident would pick up a pinch of the spilt salt and toss it over his left shoulder – a tradition still followed by some people today. In Leonardo da Vinci's painting of the Last Supper the artist has depicted Judas just after he has knocked over the salt cellar, signifying both his corruption and an ill omen for the future. Salt was also seen by some as a cure against poison, and so some politicians would eat it automatically with every meal. This custom gives us a phrase meaning you can accept something while acknowledging it might not be perfect: TAKE IT WITH A PINCH OF SALT.

Romans were very fond of herb leaves, lettuce, etc. with a liberal sprinkling of salt. They called it *herba salata;* we know it – even without the salt! – as SALAD or GREEN SALAD. One of their favourite sauces was made with lots of salt and garlic: SALSA. In fact, Italians still call salted pork sausages SALSICCIA and SALAMI, as seen on Italian menus. In fact, salt also gives us our word for minced-up salted meat – SAUSAGES – and for salty flavoured liquid served on other food: SAUCE.

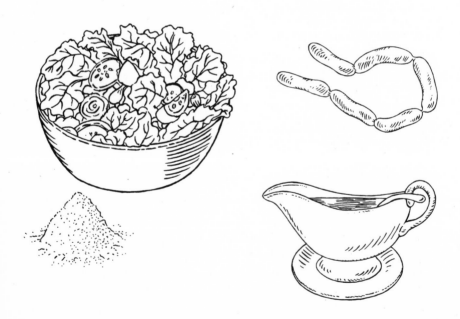

Well, I never knew that . . .
. . . the Romans invented the salad-to-go

Rome was a unique city in many ways, one of which is that it was the first city in the world to have over a million inhabitants – roughly half of whom were slaves. In fact, it was not until the 19th century that another city achieved the one million milestone. That city was LONDON. Rome's massive population resulted in a shortage of space, and so many buildings, even in the poorer parts of the city, were multi-storey. All of these tenement blocks were substantially made from wood and so were at great risk of fire, especially in the long, hot and dry summers of Italy. As a result it was forbidden to light fires in many of them, which of course made cooking impossible. As a result many people ate out or bought TAKEAWAY FOOD. Indeed, there were literally thousands of such takeaway stores around the city selling thick soups, stews and, given the Romans' predilection for salty food, a variety of salty snacks.

Charta was the Latin word for paper. Now, at the time of the Roman Empire such paper was made from wetted papyrus leaves hammered together and left to dry. It would be another thousand years before the Chinese secret invention of cellulose-based paper (i.e. paper as we know it) came to Europe. This papyrus was thick and inflexible, and over time *charta* has given us the word CARD, while its use for map-making gives us the terms for maps, CHARTS, and for

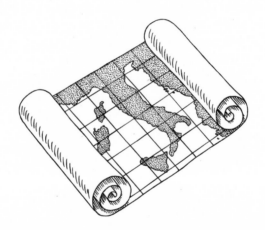

mapmakers, CARTOGRAPHERS – and, indeed, for important documents that would have been written on large sheets of paper: CHARTERS. In business there is always the temptation for suppliers to get together and come up with price-fixing deals. These would often be secretly written down on a *charta* to clarify the exact details, and so we get the term CARTEL. Also, the idea of going in to a restaurant and ordering food to be especially cooked for you but chosen from a list of options written on a card gives us the term À LA CARTE. The usual alternative, incidentally, is choosing something that originally had already been cooked and was being served to the host: TABLE D'HÔTE – literally, (from) the host's table. **WINKT!**

APPENDIX I

Bonus extract taken from
WHAT EVER HAPPENED TO OUR 27TH LETTER?
Well, I Never Knew That!
KNOWLEDGE, AND HOW WE USE IT!
ISBN 978-0-9551525-7-3

Roman Numerals

The Romans gave us the numerals
named after them, millions and seconds
– but had no idea about nothing!

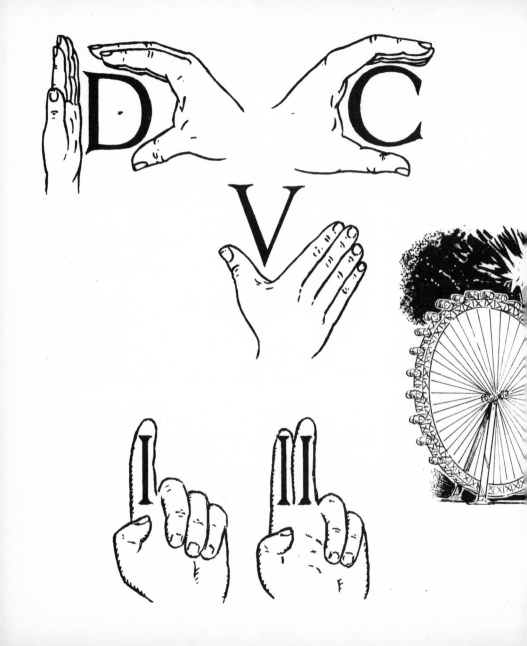

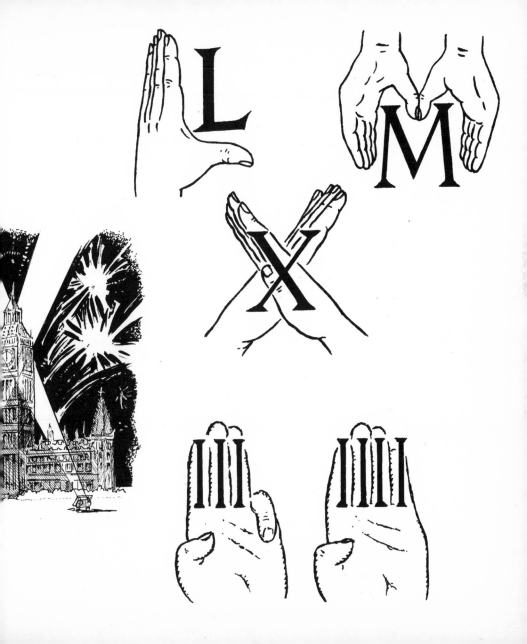

Well, I never knew that . . .
. . . you've got to hand it to the Romans for counting

The Roman numerals with which we are all familiar were directly derived from counting on fingers, with the proviso that they also needed to be easy to carve in stone and scrape in wax. Hence the symbol for one is simply a straight vertical line, representing one finger. Similarly for two, three and four. When opening the thumb to count five the shape of the hand becomes 'V'-shaped; hence the Roman numeral for 5 is V. In the same way, counting above five simply involves the addition of more lines, representing fingers on the second hand, until another V is formed. Symbolically, two hands can be combined to form X, representing

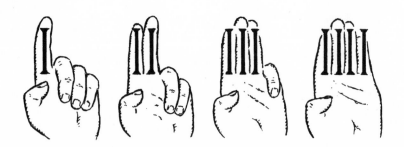

10. Interestingly, the symbol for 50 can also be formed with one hand, L, as can the symbol for 100, C. Similarly, the symbol for 500 is D. It was only later that a shorthand version of higher numbers came into use to save time and space on inscriptions, so that, for example, VIIII became IX – something that cannot be done with fingers! To represent much larger numbers the Romans simply put a straight line above the normal symbol, and this then represented 1,000 times that value: so 5,000 was written as $\overline{V}$.

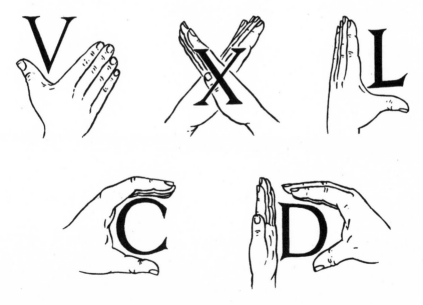

In America, some early $10 notes had the Roman numeral X printed on them, instead of the normal 10. Some $20 bills had two: XX. The slang for dollar was 'buck'; so, given that many sawing horses (supports for resting timber on while it is being cut) were made with two crossed pieces of wood at each end to provide sturdy legs, these bills became known as 'sawbucks' and 'double sawbucks' – nicknames still used today!

When Roman numerals came to Britain, they were individually named by the Anglo-Saxon words already in use (one, two, three, etc.). The only  exception was for a thousand thousands (a number not much needed in Britain at that time!) for which the Latin word was retained: MILLION, from *mille*, 'a thousand'. Incidentally, the reason why *mille* was used, even though it meant 1,000, is that a million was written as $\overline{\text{M}}$. *Mille* also gives us the word for a distance of measure originally meaning a thousand paces: a MILE.

The Anglo-Saxon words for the 'ordinal' numbers (first, third, fifth, etc.) were also used, but with one exception. The Saxon name for the ordinal number after 'first' was 'other' – the sequence went first, other, third, fourth, etc. This was simply too confusing for the Normans when they took over the country in the 11th century, so they changed this (and only this one) from the Saxon 'other' to the Latin word *seconde* – our SECOND.

When the Arabs invaded southern Europe during the 8th and 9th centuries they brought with them the number symbols that had originated in India – 1, 2, 3, 4, etc. – and over the next 300 years these gradually replaced the Roman numerals. These numerals were called ARABIC NUMERALS, and with them came the concept of the decimal point and a small symbol that had gargantuan implications for science and our modern world – ZERO!

It is fascinating to think that the Romans did not use the concept of zero at all and therefore had no symbol or numeral for it either. Indeed, they even defined the year Rome was founded as YEAR ONE (what we call 753 BC), not YEAR ZERO as you might expect. And when they reset the calendar based upon their estimate of when Jesus was born they defined the year of his birth as AD 1. Similarly, the year before AD 1 is not year zero but 1 BC. Hence, in theory at least, if someone was born in 1 BC their first birthday would be in AD 1. Compare this to someone born in 1999: their first birthday would be in 2000, and the same day in 2001 would be their SECOND birthday.

Another implication of having no year 0 is that we celebrated the new millennium on the wrong year! Think about it. The first year according to the Roman calendar ended at the end of year one. So the 2,000th year ended at the end of year 2000 – *not* at the end of 1999, as most of the world assumed!

Another implication of having no zero meant that the Romans had no mathematical symbol for MINUS. Also, the difficulty of multiplying two numbers – think of trying to calculate CLIX by MLXXV – meant they had no symbol of multiplication or division either! In fact it would be over 1,000 years after the fall of Rome before these mathematical symbols appeared in a form that we would recognize today. **WINKT!**

APPENDIX II

Bonus extract taken from
DID COWBOYS INVENT BRANDING?
Well, I Never Knew That!
BIG BUSINESS AND GREAT BRANDS
ISBN 978-0-9551525-4-2

Money and Business in Ancient Rome

Power and money have always gone
together with business – and the Romans
knew how to do all three!

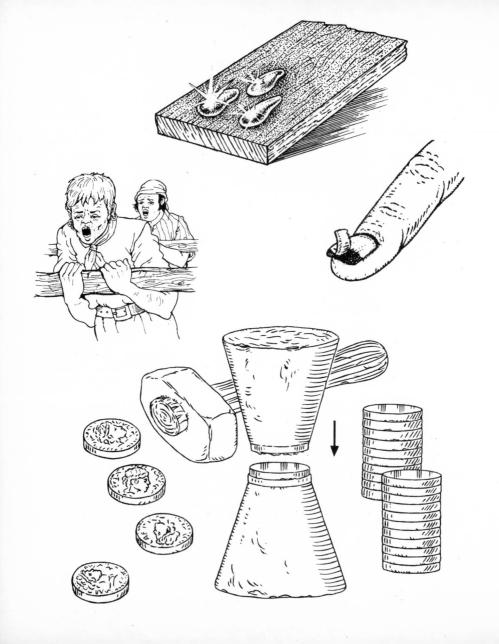

Well, I never knew that . . .
. . . money is a drug, and we owe that to the Romans

In 344 BC the Gauls attacked and sacked Rome. Afterwards the Romans prayed for help from their goddess, Juno, and received advice via her priests. The Romans asked Juno to act as an adviser and to warn them of future attacks. Over time their fortunes changed and they began to win battles again. In appreciation they built a new temple to the goddess Juno and called it the temple of 'Juno Moneta', meaning 'Juno the adviser' (using the word from which we get 'monitor'). They later established a factory to make coins right next to the temple and the coins became known as MONEY. The factory became known as the Moneta – what we call a MINT.

The reason why the coins gave their name to money is that the Romans had no concept of paper money. Nor did they use metal tokens with a low actual metal value to represent high monetary values as we do, with for example, a pound coin whose metal content is worth far less than £1. Instead the value of Roman coins was based upon the actual value of the metal (often silver) that was in them.

Cuneus is Latin for 'wedge', which was the shape of the stamping dies used to imprint metal discs to turn them into legal tender. Hence the word initially for the die and subsequently for the money: COIN. By analogy with the widespread use of coins, when we make a new form of words that becomes commonly used, or simply use such words, we are said to COIN A PHRASE. Also, anything that becomes popular or widely used can be said to GAIN CURRENCY.

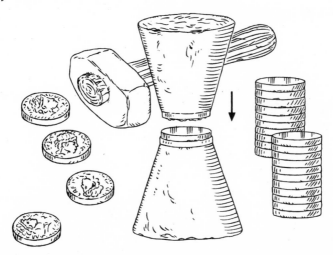

Before the British currency was decimalized in 1971 it was made up of pounds, shillings and pence. The symbols of these three units of currency were £, s and d. All three derive from ancient Rome. Bizarrely, though, the 's', which was the symbol used to represent 'shillings', was *not* in fact derived from the word shilling! Let's find out why.

The original small silver Roman coin was defined as being worth 10 asses (*denarii*). Over centuries this word *denarii* evolved into the English word PENNY. Hence the English symbol for an old (pre-decimalization) penny: 'D', for *denarii*, as in 3d meaning threepence.

The Romans also had a coin worth approximately 12 pennies. This was used in paying members of the Roman army. Like many other armies, the troops often went for long periods without receiving their pay, getting only promises instead of

 solid coins. So they called the coin SOLIDUS. This gave the middle initial 's' in £ s d. Incidentally, it was because of the name given to these coins and the troops' love of

them that the men of the army became known as SOLDIERS. However, during the Middle Ages the *solidus* coin fell out of use.

In the Carolingian Empire – named after Charles the Great, Carolus Magnus or, as we know him, CHARLEMAGNE – coins were standardized, with the weight of each silver penny being redefined by dividing one pound in weight (*libra* in Latin) of silver into 240 pennies (240 is a great number for money and trade because it can be easily divided into 1/2, 1/3, 1/4, 1/5, 1/6, 1/8, 1/10, 1/12, 1/16, 1/20, 1/24, 1/30, 1/40, 1/48, 1/60, 1/80, 1/120 and 1/240!). This is why 240 pennies were called ONE POUND. And this is why we ended up with the abbreviations for a pound of money, L or £ (as in £ s d – *libra, solidus, denarii*) and a pound in weight, LB (*libra*).

Incidentally, the idea of *libra* being a unit of weight led to the idea of two equal weights balancing each other, giving us the word EQUILIBRIUM.

In the ancient world this next word was originally a unit of weight that was used extensively throughout the Mediterranean by merchants, among other things for weighing silver coins. It then came to be used to describe a certain value of money, in the same way that our word 'pound' came to mean both a defined unit of weight and nowadays the value of 100 pennies. However, this word then began to be associated with the payment of money to craftsmen and other skilled individuals. Over time the word then became associated with the skill itself, which is how the word is most commonly used today: TALENT.

Lucrum was Latin for both profit and greed. This gives us the word for a profitable venture – LUCRATIVE – and the slang for money, LUCRE (filthy or otherwise!).

The Latin word for a small leather bag was *bulga*. These little bags were often used for holding money, and as the Romans had no concept of paper money they would quickly fill up with coins. From the resulting shape we get the word BULGE. Incidentally, by the 17th century the cross-section of a galleon was pear-shaped, with a 'bulge' around the waterline. This was designed to stop ships being top-heavy and overturning. However, all ships at this age leaked, and so pumps were installed on the deck that was at the waterline so that water could be pumped from the bottom of the ship up and out over the side. Because these pumps were at the *bulge* of the ship, they became known as bulge pumps or BILGE PUMPS. The mucky water that they removed was called BILGE – and hence the term meaning unwanted, unusable and horribly mucky: A LOAD OF BILGE.

When someone went out to buy things they would only be able to spend what they had with them in their *bulga*. Over time this word evolved to give us a modern term meaning the amount of money that you can spend: BUDGET.

Throughout history money and power have always gone together, and so, using the Latin word *caput* meaning head, we get the word for the money that gives the *head* person his power: CAPITAL. Now, in early society livestock was the ultimate measure of resources, and therefore wealth was measured in the number of 'heads' of cows a person possessed; and so over time the word 'capital' evolved to describe the largest livestock: cows or CATTLE. This word also evolved to give us another term referring to livestock – CHATTELS, and the phrase for all your portable wealth: GOODS AND CHATTELS. Over time this term even came to include also a man's wife, on the basis that in those days wives were effectively the property of their husbands.

Well, I never knew that . . .
. . . a little box could take all your money

The Roman word for a 'box' was *capsa*. This has given us many modern words: for example, a very small box or container often used to store or deliver something, CAPSULE; and the word for a little house, *casa*, which in turn was used to describe a secret room within a house in which illegal gambling could take place: CASINO. It also gives us the word for a storage box that can be used for moving things around: CASE. Where briefing papers are being moved it is called a BRIEFCASE, and where suits or other clothes are involved it is called a SUITCASE. The verb to surround something with a protective 'box' is to ENCASE it. The term for a wooden frame around the panes of a glass window is a CASEMENT.

Now, an obvious use of boxes is for the storage of money, and so again from the word *capsa* we get our term that originally referred to the box of money and then later came to be used for the coins themselves: CASH.

The idea of putting something in a box to hold it for safe keeping led to the verb *capere* meaning 'to hold'. This gives us the words to describe the act of catching hold of someone –

CAPTURE – and then to describe them once they are caught: CAPTIVE. Policemen, whose job it was to grab criminals, were given a slang name based on the same root: COPPER. On board ship the mechanism that 'holds' the anchor rope and then winds it in is called the CAPSTAN.

Mercis was Latin for 'goods'. From this we get the terms for the trading of goods, MERCANTILE, and for the people who trade in goods, MERCHANTS. Those who specialize in trading in cloth or related items were called MERCERS. The places where merchants used to gather together to trade became known as MARKETS. The Romans named their god of merchants MERCURY. This god was also the mischievous messenger of the gods who had a fun-loving, unpredictable character. Hence someone with this sort of character can be referred to as MERCURIAL.

In the Middle Ages the word 'quick' meant 'alive'. Hence we get the phrase describing all people whether they are alive or not: THE QUICK AND THE DEAD. From the same origin we get the name for the living skin underneath fingernails that is very sensitive if exposed, QUICK, and in turn the phrase meaning to go straight to a sensitive subject: TO CUT TO THE QUICK. The word was also used to describe a section of ground that appeared to eat up people and animals who tried to cross it as

if it were alive: QUICKSAND. A shiny liquid metal that moved as if it were alive was QUICKSILVER. The fact that this liquid is so difficult to control and seems to flow wherever it wants to led to it being called a mercurial liquid and then simply MERCURY. The link to silver then resulted in the silvery planet nearest

the sun, which can appear to the naked eye as a very bright silvery star, being named MERCURY.

Going back to the original meaning of *mercis* as 'goods' gives us the name of soldiers who fight only in return for goods or the money to buy goods: MERCENARIES; and also the word that originally meant providing goods to someone even though there is no need to do so: MERCY.

Adding the prefix 'com' which means 'together' we get the word for trading goods among two or more people: COMMERCE. Incidentally, the Latin term for essential goods was *communis*. Karl Marx believed these should be shared by all of society, rather than unfairly distributed with the rich getting the best. This gave him the idea for the term COMMUNISM.

Consumo was Latin for 'to eat', and so we get the words CONSUME and CONSUMER.

In 390 BC the Roman army was defeated by an army of barbarian Gauls (ancestors of the French) and Rome was sacked. The defeat was blamed upon the old, inflexible style of fighting based upon the Greek formation called by a word meaning 'finger', referring to the rows of soldiers: PHALANX (our finger bones are still called phalanges). The Romans split the large phalanx into smaller independent units of around 160 men and called these units a 'hand full' of men. In Latin *mano* means hand and *plere* means fill, and so we get MANIPLE. Hence something that can be moved easily using one's hands is MANIPULATED. A body of soldiers that can be moved in a coordinated way can be MANOEUVRED. Interestingly, when *mano* is combined with a version of the Latin word *equus* for horse we get the Roman term for people who handled horses: *manoeggiare*, or, as we know them, MANAGERS.

The Latin word for 'plunge' was *mergo*, which give us the words for going under (*sub*) the surface – being SUBMERGED – and for being under the water, having plunged in: IMMERSED. We also get the idea of throwing one liquid – or company – into another and seeing if they combine: MERGER.

When selling something, you hand goods over to the buyer

and what comes back to you is money. Using the Latin words *venio* meaning 'come' and *re* meaning 'back', we get the word REVENUE (literally, 'come-back').

Roman doctors were surprisingly knowledgeable about how the human body worked, if for no other reason than that the state employed over 300,000 soldiers and needed to know how to deal with their injuries and ailments. The Latin word for caring was *cura*, from which we get the word CURE. Combining this with the prefix *se-* which means 'without' gives us the word meaning without a care or, in the modern sense, safe: SECURE. This also gives us the term for 'safe' financial instruments traded in the City of London: SECURITIES.

Well, I never knew that . . .
. . . if you gave short measures the courts would size you up

A commonly used measure of weight in ancient Rome was named after a very common beast of burden: the AS, named after the ass. Because it was such a commonly used weight it became associated with the word 'one', and by the Middle

Ages the word was used both for the one on a dice and for the one in playing cards: ACE. Originally 'ace' had a connotation of low value. However, as new card games defined an ace as the top card in a suit, the word came to stand for 'the best'. By the First World War it was initially used to describe the number one fighter pilot of each

squadron, although by the end of the war it was used of any pilot who had shot down a certain number of enemy planes: FIGHTER ACE. It was then incorporated into tennis to describe how a player wins a point by playing only one stroke: SERVING AN ACE.

The Romans split the *as* unit of weight into 12 parts called *uncia*. From this we get the word for the subdivision of our pound weight, OUNCE, although of course we have 16 ounces in a pound. This is because traders found 12 ounces a difficult number, as halving and re-halving produce, which was very common, resulted in 6, 3, then $1\frac{1}{2}$, then $\frac{3}{4}$, whereas the number 16 could be repeatedly halved to 8, 4, 2, 1 before reaching difficult fractions. Over time, therefore, the pound was split into 16 parts, giving us 16 ounces in one pound.

A similar issue arose with the common measure of 100 pounds, or, as we know it, a HUNDREDWEIGHT – often written in shorthand using C, the Roman numeral for 100: CWT. Dividing this unit into eighths and sixteenths was too frustrating, and over time the basis of the hundredweight changed. This time, though, instead of it being split into more,

smaller parts (like the pound), additional pounds were added on, so that in Britain a hundredweight became 112 pounds – a number that can easily be divided by 2, 4, 8 and 16. However, in the 18th century the newly independent America decided to reinforce its rejection of Britain by returning to the original measure of 100 pounds. In the meantime a ton had already been defined as 20 hundredweight – so that a US ton became 2,000 pounds, while a British ton remained 2,240 pounds! And that is how it still stands to this day!   **WINKT!**

Bonus extract taken from
DO SPIES WIN OLYMPIC MEDALS?
Well, I Never Knew That!
SPORT, GAMES AND GAMBLING

Gladiators and other Roman Sports

The Romans worked hard and fought hard,
but they played even harder!

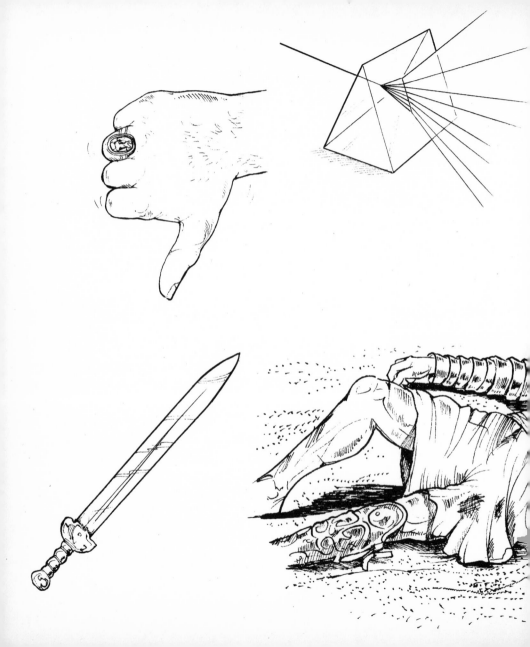

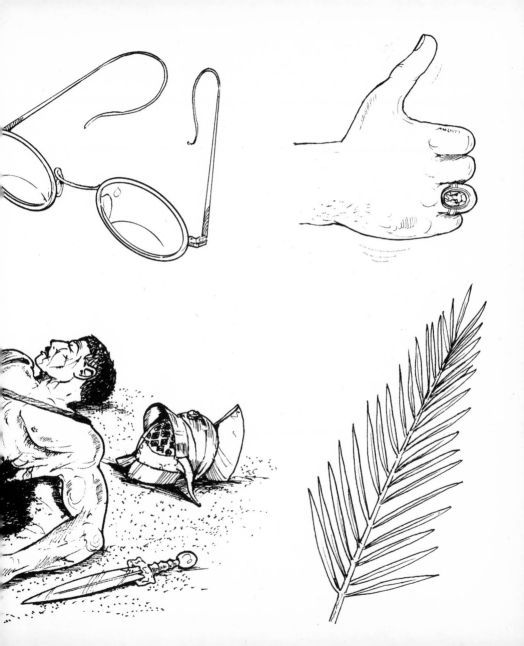

Well, I never knew that . . .
. . . some Roman ladies gave gladiators the thumbs up

Roman generals armed their soldiers with the famous short stabbing sword – the gladius. They did this to stop them taking wild swings and instead make them operate as a team stabbing out from behind a wall of shields into the exposed armpits of their enemies who were taking big swings. There is even conjecture that some generals did not allow their soldiers to sharpen the sides of their blades, further discouraging any cutting swings. This was also the sword often used in arenas when slaves fought each other to the death. These competitors were named after the sword: GLADIATORS.

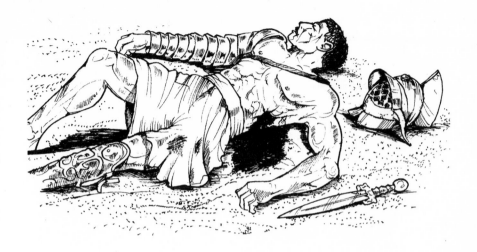

Many of these gladiators were criminals, prisoners of war or simply people who had fallen out with the emperor. They would be shoved into the arena and have to fight for their lives in a bizarre range of contests. Christians were often pitted against wild animals such as lions or even maddened elephants from North Africa. Incidentally, the Romans called black panthers 'pards'. They also assumed that the animals that resembled yellow lions but had black spots on them were in fact a cross between lions and panthers. Hence the name that we still use: LEOPARDS.

Sometimes one man would be made to wear a helmet with no eye-holes so that he could not see his opponent. Sometimes women would be set against dwarves. One emperor even personally fought against opponents who were weakened through drugs and lack of food and had to use weapons made of lead so that they could hardly be picked up! He is recorded has having had over 200 successful fights!

There were also professional gladiators trained to use specific sets of weapons, who would rarely be killed simply because they cost so much to train and look after. A few of these would become celebrities, like modern-day football stars, and occasionally would earn their freedom by being so popular that they were liberated by the Emperor. These gladiators were fine physical specimens and would often attract rich female admirers who would visit the gladiatorial barracks for a 'bit of rough' and pay for the privilege.

If two professional gladiators gave a good display of skilled and exciting fighting the crowd would give a symbol that the loser should be spared. The ultimate decision was made by the Emperor, who would often assess the mood of the audience and then usually follow their lead. To save someone he would make a fist with his right hand held sideways and then extend his thumb, which then became representative of the victorious gladiators sword. He would then twist his wrist to make his thumb point either upwards, meaning he would live, or downwards, meaning the sword should be thrust into the losing gladiator's heart. Hence we get the gesture and verbal expression: THUMBS UP – and, of course, THUMBS DOWN!

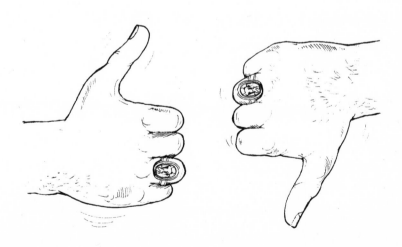

Well, I never knew that . . .

. . . the Romans gave us Oxford Circus!

Ruling the Roman Empire was obviously a very difficult business, and the emperors consistently feared uprisings and coups that would oust them, almost certainly with calamitous results for both them and their families. The commentator Juvenal said in the 2nd century that there are primarily two things an emperor has to give the population to keep it happy: food, and thrilling entertainment such as chariot races and gladiator games, which would take place in round amphitheatres called *circuses*. Hence the phrase meaning giving people basic food and entertainment to keep them from thinking about other more important things: BREAD AND CIRCUSES. This is where we get the term for a show involving horses and other acts going around and around an arena to entertain the audience: CIRCUS. It is also why many junctions in central London, where at some time in the past there has been some form of roundabout, are also called circuses. Examples include Oxford Circus, where Oxford Street intersects with Regent Street, and

Cambridge Circus, where Shaftesbury Avenue and other roads intersect.

The Latin word for 'sand' has given us an alternative name for a sports stadium. Originally, however, it was applied only to those amphitheatres where gladiators or Christians would be killed in large numbers, and where in fact the sand was needed to soak up the blood: ARENA (Latin for 'sand').

In ancient Rome, palm leaves were a sign of deep respect and admiration. This is why Jesus' path into Jerusalem was paved with palm leaves, giving the Christian celebration of

PALM SUNDAY. Equally a victorious gladiator would be given a palm leaf in recognition of his achievement. Hence the expression TO BEAR A PALM. Notable gladiators could eventually win their freedom, and this would be signified by the award of a *rudis*, a wooden sword. But many of these gladiators still went on taking part in the contests, not wanting to give up the fame, the lifestyle and the buzz of the adrenalin rush.

Well, I never knew that . . .
. . . the Romans gave us spectacles!

Towards the end of the Roman Empire the sport of charioteering became an obsession with many people. In fact the Circus Maximus was a specially built racing circuit designed to accommodate over 200,000 people – around 15 per cent of the entire population of Rome. Initially there were two teams: *russata* (red) and *albata* (white). When the contests were expanded to include two more chariots per race, the *passina* (green) and *veneta* (blue) teams emerged. This sport became far more important than football or Formula One in contemporary British society and led to political affiliations and vicious riots. The word used to describe these various teams has come to be used in political and other arenas in the modern world: FACTIONS. In fact the rioting and disquiet caused by these warring factions was a contributor to the overall decline and fall of the Roman Empire. Now there's a warning for football fans!

The arenas that were specially built for these races, in which the chariots were drawn by horses, were often named after the Greek word for horse, *hippos*, and *dromos*, meaning 'course': HIPPODROME. The association with large crowds, excitement and big venues has led to old-style music halls, theatres and night clubs adopting this name. Many of them in fact took the name of the world's largest ever 'colossal' arena for gladiatorial combat: THE COLOSSEUM, often spelt COLISEUM.

 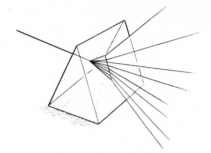

Spectare, meaning to watch, has given us our words for people who watch, SPECTATORS, and for devices to help us watch, SPECTACLES; also for the splitting of light into its full range of colours, SPECTRUM, and hence for a full set of variations of anything: FULL SPECTRUM. Then again, there is our word for a 'must-see event', A SPECTACLE, which will inevitably prove to be SPECTACULAR. The viewing of something from a particular angle gives us the word ASPECT. Combining *spectare* with the prefix *sub-* meaning 'under', we get the word meaning someone who appears to be taking a sneaky look at something: SUSPECT (subspect); and anyone who suspects someone else is SUSPICIOUS. **WINKT!**

APPENDIX IV

Bonus extract taken from
IS ASTROLOGY A LOAD OF CASTOR AND POLLUX?
Well, I Never Knew That!
TIME, ASTRONOMY AND ASTROLOGY
ISBN 978-0-9551525-8-0

From the First Calendar to Leap Years

Ancient Greeks, Sumerians, Romans, the Popes . . . everyone seems to have had a go at regulating time by adjusting the calendar, and all their efforts have left traces in the systems and words we use today.

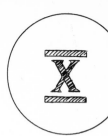

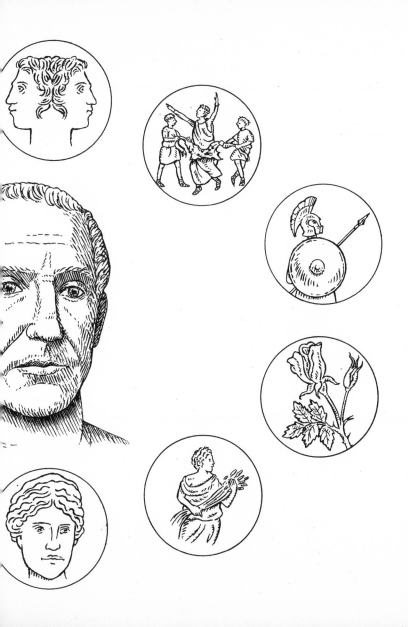

Well, I never knew that . . .
. . . some ancient calendars went round in circles

The ancient Sumerians were one of the earliest people to conduct significant trade and commerce. As a result they developed a numbering system based around the number sixty (versus our system based around the number ten, *decem* in Latin, giving us the term DECIMAL). This is because 60 is easily divisible by so many numbers: 2, 3, 4, 5, 6, 10, 12, 15, 20 and of course 60. This makes splitting numbers into fractions very easy. (Try splitting 10 into 6ths, or 12ths and you will see their point!) This system is called the sexagesimal numbering system.

Now, the Sumerians knew there were about 360 days in a year and in fact used a calendar of 12 months of 30 days with occasional extra days to try to keep the calendar in line with the seasons. They therefore linked the number 360 with the circular path of the sun, especially as this fitted into their sexagesimal numbering system of 6 × 60. Subsequently they defined any full circle as having 360 DEGREES. (Incidentally, the

Sumerians were not just interested in circles for esoteric reasons – after all, they did invent the wheel!) Using the sexagesimal system again they also split each 360th of a circle (i.e. one degree) into 60 parts. The Romans later called each of these subdivisions a 'very small' part of the full circle – in Latin, *minuta*, from which we get MINUTES, each minute being one-sixtieth of a degree. The 'second' split into 60 parts gives us the subdivision of a minute: a SECOND. We still use this sexagesimal system for describing angles throughout our mathematics of circles and angles, which itself is named, from Greek via Latin, after how we measured (*metior*) the world (*geo*): GEOMETRY.

However, the one serious problem with the Sumerian calendar was that the year of 360 days was five to six days too short! Every year, the seasons moved by approximately six days, and so extra days were needed. The Egyptians solved this problem with an agricultural calendar year based upon the very regular annual flooding of the Nile. They started each year and ended each year on the day of the flood, which gave them a year of 365 days. This was 12 months of 30 days, plus various extra 'god days' through the year. However, the priests kept a religious calendar of exactly 365 days independent of the annual flood. As the earth's rotation is approximately 365.25 days their calendar lost a day every four years. Hence their religious year and their calendar moved slowly through the seasons until 365 × 4 years (i.e. 1,460 years) had passed – when it came back into alignment again!

The Egyptians also noticed that the brightest star in the sky rose exactly in line with the sun on the first day of the flood. This is scientific coincidence, but they believed it to be very portentous. The Romans called the star Canis (dog), from an imaginary shape of a dog they could see in the stars; hence we know this as a CANICULAR YEAR. As this phenomenon coincided with the hottest time of year it was assumed that the alignment of the star and the sun caused the extra heat, and so this part of the summer was called the 'DOG DAYS' OF SUMMER, after the star Canis. Incidentally, the modern name for this star is Sirius, which in Latin means SCORCHING. The Egyptians called the star Sothis, and hence we know their calendar system as the SOTHIC CALENDAR.

The Jewish calendar starts with the year when the world was created. According to the Jewish interpretation of the scriptures, this was 3761 BC, making AD 2006 equivalent to their year 5766. This calendar is also a lunar-based calendar, with each month either 29 or 30 days long. As there are 12 cycles of the moon every year, this means the Jewish 'lunar' year is shorter than the solar year of 365.25 days. Hence, occasionally extra months need to be inserted to keep the dates of key festivals, such as gathering in the harvest, in line with the seasons. From the Greek word *embolein* meaning to insert (from which we get the word for a blood vessel that is blocked by an 'inserted' blood clot or air bubble: EMBOLISM) we get the term for the years in which extra months are inserted: EMBOLISMIC YEARS.

Well, I never knew that . . .
. . . the Romans first began the year with war

When the ancient Italian hero Romulus founded a great city in 753 BC it was named after him: ROME. The Roman calendar originally started from the year when Rome was officially founded, which the Romans defined as 1 AUC (having no concept of the number zero). AUC was short for *ab urbe condita*, meaning 'from the founding'. Like all other Roman writing, this was always written in block capitals (because no one had invented small letters), which is also why AD AND BC ARE ALWAYS WRITTEN AS BLOCK CAPITALS.

Romulus applied the Latin love of decimalization to the calendar and defined a year as TEN MONTHS LONG. The start of the year was defined as the spring solstice – what we call 21 March. The Romans named the first month of their new calendar after the god who was supposed to be the father of Romulus and also god of forests, sylvan woods, fields and agriculture: MARS SYLVANUS. However, the Romans quickly became embroiled in several wars and needed a warlike deity. As Mars was already a key god, they chose to give him an additional role, that of GOD OF WAR, based upon the Greek god of war, ARES. From then on Mars had two roles – Mars Sylvanus and Mars Gradivus. Over time, the war-god version became dominant and the name of the month was shortened to simply MARS – later our month of MARCH.

The second month was named from the Latin word *aperire*, 'to open', referring to buds opening in spring: APRIL. The third month, when spring is well under way, was named after Maius, the Goddess of Growth: MAY. The fourth was named after the Queen of the Gods, Juno: JUNE. The next six months were named using simple numbers: 5, 6, 7, 8, 9, 10 – Quintilis, Sextilis and then SEPTEMBER, OCTOBER, NOVEMBER, DECEMBER.

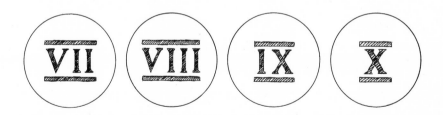

However, a calendar that matched neither the moon nor the sun quickly fell out of synchronization with the seasons and the monthly cycles, and so was useless for a mainly agricultural society. So before long two more months were added to the end of the year to make the calendar work.

According to legend, the illegitimate son of the Greek god Apollo fell out with the gods and was cursed with having to guard the gateway into heaven. To help him he was given a face on both sides of his head. He was named after the word for door, *ianus* or, as we know him, JANUS ('i' and 'j' were the same letter in these days). He eventually travelled to Italy, where he had a son called Tiberius. This boy drowned in a river that then took his name: the RIVER TIBER.

When Rome was founded Janus became the Roman god of gateways, with a festival just after the winter solstice which was seen as the 'gateway' to longer days and springtime. In his honour a tradition developed that during this festival people looked back over the previous seasons and forward over the coming seasons. The idea of having two faces and so being able to say one thing to one person while simultaneously saying something else to another gives us the phrase JANUS-FACED and the more common version TWO-FACED.

In fact, Janus was chosen by Romulus as one of the key gods for the Romans, and on one occasion is supposed to have saved Rome from an enemy attack by making a hot spring appear at the top of a hill and pour down, killing many of the attacking army and sending the others fleeing away. In thanks for this, a temple was built to Janus and the door was always left open in time of war so that if Janus wished to come out and help he could release another stream of boiling water.

It also meant that soldiers returning from war could enter either to thank the god for victory and celebrate a new beginning of Roman rule, or to seek consolation for failure and pray to be reinvigorated to resume the fight. From the founding of Rome in 753 BC to the inauguration of the first emperor, Augustus, in 27 BC (over 700 years) the doors were closed just once! This was for part of 241 BC, after the Romans had defeated the Carthaginians in the first Punic War.

An annual feast was already established a few weeks after the winter solstice, once the trend of longer days had become noticeable. So when an extra month was introduced around the time of this festival it simply took the name of the god whose festival it was: JANUARIUS – from Janus – giving us our month JANUARY.

There was also a springtime pagan festival of purification in Rome that involved sacrificing rams and then, after certain rituals had been conducted, cutting their skins into strips called *febria*. These would be drawn over the priests to cover them in blood, after which they would run through the streets holding the bloody strips. As the ram was a long-established symbol of fertility, these strips were considered to be cures for infertility and to increase sexual performance, and so men and

women would often run up and touch them. This month was therefore named after the ceremony of these strips: FEBRUARY.

Well, I never knew that . . .
. . . there were no weeks in the first calendars

A communication from the emperor in Rome would often begin *Data Romae*, meaning 'given at Rome' followed by the day it was written. Over the years this evolved into the single word for a particular day: DATE. Subsequently the idea of a lovers' tryst being arranged on a particular day has given us the terms DATE and DATING.

On the first day of every month in ancient Rome, a group of specially selected priests and senators would publicly proclaim the important dates for that month (i.e. the new moon, holidays, etc.). From the Latin word *calare* meaning 'to proclaim', this day came to be known as Calends. This was also the day upon which loan repayments or interest instalments would typically be due. Thus a book that set out a schedule of repayments falling due over a period of several months became known by a word subsequently used to describe any book showing several months of time: a CALENDAR.

Incidentally, a plant whose extract was used to help women with regular painful monthly periods was called CALENDULA.

At the start of every month the relevant information for that month was made public by being posted on a large white board in the forum, and at other public places. These boards were called *albus*, meaning 'white' (from which we also get ALBINO). Subsequently, the idea was applied to large books with white pages designed to keep copies of documents and in which monks could record psalms and other pieces of information. This concept was then extended to keeping reference collections of dried plants for herbal medicines, and more recently for collectable items such as stamps. During the 1960s the idea of collections resulted in the word being applied to music records, and more recently to CDs, which – even though the original reason for the name no longer applies – are still called ALBUMS.

The same group of priests and senators that proclaimed key dates was also responsible for adding or subtracting days to try to keep the calendar in step with the seasons. This role would often be abused for personal gain, for example to shorten a political enemy's term in office or to lengthen the period of a commercial contract. Indeed, the Senate carefully guarded the knowledge associated with the art and science behind the calendrical system so that they could abuse it. So careful were they to protect their secret that disclosing any knowledge about how the system worked was a crime punishable by death.

In the early days of Rome there was no concept of a week. Instead, the month was divided into three parts. The first five to seven days were called Calends (after the name of the first day), the next eight to nine were called Nones (Roman for nine) and the rest were called Ides. In the Roman calendar the 15th days of March, May, July, and October were called the Ides; in other months it was the 13th day. This structure was still in use in places right through to the late Middle Ages in Europe, so the Elizabethan audience in England would have understood the famous warning in Shakespeare's play *Julius Caesar*, 'BEWARE THE IDES OF MARCH' – meaning 15 March, that is, the first day of the Ides. The 16th was called the second ides, the 17th the third ides, and so on.

As feast days were typically driven by holy and religious dates they were also referred to as holy days, a term which evolved to give us HOLIDAY. Most holy days would involve some form of festival or celebration. The word we use to describe events of this kind comes from the Latin word for holidays, *feriae*: FAIR.

Well, I never knew that . . .
. . . Caesar leaped ahead with calendar reform

When Julius Caesar returned from his famous conquest of Gaul he camped his army on the northern bank of a river just to the north of Rome. There was an ancient law, designed to avoid the danger of a military coup, that forbade any general to bring his army any closer to the city than the banks of this river. However, after much thought Caesar decided to take the risk, march south, and attack his erstwhile friend but now enemy, Pompey. To do this he had to do something that now means metaphorically to take a hugely important and irreversible step: CROSS THE RUBICON.

Pompey fled, pursued by Caesar and his army, eventually to Egypt where he was betrayed, killed and decapitated, after which his embalmed head was delivered to Caesar – nice! It was here that Caesar met two critical people. One was a beautiful, ethnically Greek, princess (descended from Alexander the Great's right-hand man, Ptolemy) whom he fell in love with and married, despite the fact he already had a wife in Rome. Her name was CLEOPATRA. The second was an astronomer called Sosigenes who explained to him that although the official religious Egyptian calendar had a year of 365 days, in fact Egyptian scholars had shown that the year was $365\frac{1}{4}$ days long. It had been only the priests who had refused to accept they were wrong, preventing Egypt from correcting their own calendar centuries before and avoiding an increasingly compounding problem.

Caesar was fascinated, and when he returned to Rome he introduced a new calendar based on this principle. His solution was to make a one-off correction to bring the calendar back into phase with the seasons, adding an extra day every four years – hence creating the first LEAP YEAR. This extra day was added at the very end of the calendar year, which at this time was FEBRUARY. He also adjusted the length of each month to ensure that alternate months had 30 and then 31 days. The only exception was the very last month (February), which could only have 29 days to give a total of 365 days. It would then have 30 days in a leap year. In his honour this is now known as the JULIAN CALENDAR, and was in use across Europe for over 1,500 years. However, its introduction caused chaos, as it was necessary for the year 46 BC to have 445 days; and so this year was known as *ultimus annus confusionis* (the year of ultimate confusion). Interestingly, Egypt, which technically was not part of the Roman Empire, held on to its old 365-day calendar until Caesar's successor invaded Egypt 16 years later and forced the new calendar upon them, despite continuing opposition from their priests. The start of the year was also redefined as the first day of the month starting nearest to the winter solstice – 1 JANUARY.

When the start of the year was fixed at 1 January, the Janus festival tradition of looking backwards and forwards shifted to the night before that day: NEW YEAR'S EVE, when people looked backwards and forward through time. Here the idea of making new commitments to the gods for the new year emerged – what we know as NEW YEAR'S RESOLUTIONS.

When Caesar was assassinated, the Senate decided he should have a month named after him. He had been born in the month of Quintilis, and so they chose to rename the month Julius (what we know as JULY – although up until the 17th century it was still pronounced as if it was the first part of his name, i.e. like the girl's name Julie). In the years following Julius Caesar's death in 44 BC, his great-nephew and adopted heir Gaius Octavianus became a very successful general and statesman, popular with the army and the people alike. He conquered Egypt, bringing the vital Egyptian wheat fields under the total control of Rome for the first time, and became the first Emperor of Rome in 27 BC. He was considered to be a very august and majestic leader and was given an appropriate honorary title meaning just that: AUGUSTUS.

As Augustus' uncle had already been honoured by having the month of Quintilis renamed Julius, and as he had followed Julius Caesar as ruler of Rome, the Senate decreed that the month following Julius, Sextilis, should be renamed after him. So henceforth it was called Augustus or, as we know it, AUGUST. However, Sextilis had only 30 days – one fewer than July – and as Octavius Augustus (as we know him) was a superb ruler and could not be insulted, the senate decided to add another day to August to make it 31 DAYS LONG. To balance the year they took this from February, which is why that month now has only 28 days (29 in a leap year). However, instead of the neat alternating 30/31 days of the months that had been designed into the Julian calendar, there were now three months of 31 days next to each other – July, August and September. Therefore the next few months were varied to re-establish alternate months of 30 and 31 days. September gave a day to October (now 31 days) and November gave one to December (now also 31 days).

Several years later, in an attempt to win favour with the next ruler, the Senate voted that this emperor, Tiberius (named after the river that flows through Rome), should also have a month named after him within his lifetime, with September becoming Tiberius. Fortunately he saw through the ploy and put a stop to it, saying that if every emperor had a month named after him they would quickly run out of months! The months have remained unchanged ever since.

Hence the childhood rhyme,

Thirty days hath September,
April, June and November,
All the rest hath thirty-one,
Save February alone.
Which hath eight days and a score,
'Til leap year gives her one day more!

Note this rhyme was written in the days when 'hath' was used instead of 'has' and also when the word 'one' was pronounced 'own' and so rhymed with 'alone'. In fact, we still have some relics of this old pronunciation in our language today: for example, the word for being sad and alone, LONELY. Similarly, the phrase 'at one with God' gave us the word ATONE, also still pronounced 'at-own'.

Now, with so much history to the establishment of our calendar you may think the story is over. However, unfortunately the Julian calendar was wrong! The net result was that the Catholic Church lost a Sunday, the Pope had to steal time, thousands of peasants revolted, the tax year moved, April Fool's Day was invented and Napoleon won a battle because his two enemies were using different calendars! But all that's another story. If you want to find out more, it is all explained in *IS ASTROLOGY A LOAD OF CASTOR AND POLLUX? Well, I Never Knew That! TIME, ASTRONOMY AND ASTROLOGY.* **WINKT!**

Thank you for reading this book. I do hope you said ...

Please read on and find out about:

- Locating your favourite phrases from the Index.
- How you can help make a brand new word.
- How to join WINKT the club.
- Other fascinating books in the series.
- 'Houston – we MAY have a problem!'
- How to discover your family's history, coat of arms and the origin of your surname.

Index

MESSAGE FROM THE AUTHOR

Please help create a brand new word!

'Well I Never Knew That!' – the story so far

Back in Victorian Dublin a man bet that he could get everyone in Dublin using a brand new word within 24 hours. He won the bet by having four letters scrawled all over the walls that night. The next morning everyone pointed at the letters, said them out loud and said, 'What is that?' The letters were Q U I Z. He had created the word QUIZ, which we now use to describe competitions where someone says – 'What is …?'

I foolishly made a similar bet in a pub – to create a brand new word and to get it into the dictionary. This turned into a gargantuan project of tracking down and linking the most intriguing, fascinating and funniest origins of everyday phrases and names in the English language. All the boring ones have been thrown away! That's how this series of books came about!

When friends read the first book they often said 'Well, I never knew that!' – hence the name of the series. Then they shortened it to WINKT – the acronym of 'Well I Never Knew That!' meaning 'Wow!' or 'Gosh!' This is the new word: 'WINKT'!!!

'Please help finish the story!'

Now you've got WINKT the book – why not help create 'WINKT' the word and finish the story! All you have to do is send an email to word@winkt.com saying that 'I think "WINKT", meaning "Wow!" or "Gosh!" should be a new word in the dictionary.'

This will be added to the petition and when we get enough you will have played your part in creating a BRAND NEW WORD in the English language! In fact, if we get more than enough, we may even get into the *Guinness Book of World Records* as the most requested word ever! And, of course, tell your friends to email in as well. The more the merrier!

As a thank you I will give you free membership of WINKT the club!
Thank you,

Now you have enjoyed a WINKT book why not join WINKT the club?

As a member you can benefit from:

- Advance information on new books before they are generally available.

- Information on other WINKT products, cards, posters, etc.

- Beautiful manuscript-style scrolls that tell the professionally researched history and heritage of your family surname together with an historically accurate full-colour coat of arms. Fascinating and eye-catching presents, either framed or unframed. We can also offer a scroll with two coats of arms – ideal for a wedding or anniversary present.

- The opportunity to get your name into the credits of a future WINKT book by offering a new WINKT expression.

- A newsletter with more fascinating derivations, members' questions, competitions and prizes.

- Occasional emails sent to you with fascinating new WINKT origins.

- Sets of approved WINKT questions for use in pub/trivia quizzes, parties or dinner parties.

- 'Ask Peter' service for the derivation of specific words or phrases.

- Join the campaign to get 'WINKT' recognized as an official word and enter the Guinness Book of World Records to get the most requested word ever!

And much, much more.

Simply register online at www.WINKT.com and get your friends and family to register too! Join the fun today!

Recommended questions for Book Circles

'Well, I Never Knew That!' books are great for book circles because they can be read a little bit at a time, are such fun and always spark off interesting questions and discussions that can cause a real stir! For example:

- Which origins most surprised you?
- Which was your most 'WINKTASTIC' moment?
- How many times did you actually say 'Well, I never knew that!'?
- Who have you shared the WINKTs with and what was their reaction?
- How many times have you noticed people using the phrases since reading the book?
- What regional or family variations in phrases have you noticed?
- What must it be like for foreigners trying to learn English?
- What phrases or expressions used by other people really annoy you?
- What different nicknames do you use for family/friends or human anatomy?
- What phrases have been used in your family for years without anyone ever challenging what they really mean or why they exist?
- What new words or phrases do children bring back from school?
- What other phrases do you now want to know the origin of?

You can always log on to www.winkt.com and simply 'Ask Peter'.

And of course if you know a really interesting origin let Peter know so he can include it in a future book and include your name in the credits!

We love hearing from book circles and so, as a thank you, we offer special discounts for book-club orders. Log on to www.winkt.com to find out more.

Other books in the WINKT series

DID NOAH INVENT TENNIS?

AN HISTORIC MISCELLANY

Do you know ...

... why we score tennis 'love, 15, 30, 40, deuce'?

... why you had better 'cut to the chase', to avoid running 'from pillar to post'?

... why getting the 'sack' is better than being 'fired'?

... why the Battle of Agincourt was such a 'cock-up' for the French?

... why the 'exception' doesn't 'prove the rule' – and never did!

ISBN 0-9551525-1-8
ISBN 978-0-9551525-1-1

WHO PUT THE 'GREAT' IN GREAT BRITAIN?

THE HISTORY OF GREAT BRITAIN

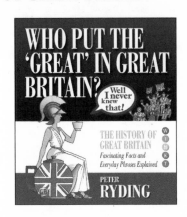

Do you know ...

... why England has three heraldic lions – because none of them was English!

... why Cromwell was such a 'whitewash', 'warts and all'?

... why we call our flag a 'Union JACK' – and why you may never have seen one?

... why a popular nursery rhyme teaches our children about destruction, boozing, pawning and child mortality? It's enough to make you 'pop your clogs'!

... and what is a 'cock-horse' anyway?

ISBN 0-9551525-3-4
ISBN 978-0-9551525-3-5

DO SPIES WIN OLYMPIC MEDALS?

SPORTS, GAMES AND GAMBLING

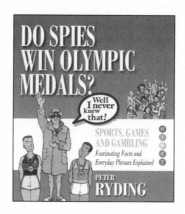

Do you know ...

... why going 'down like ninepins' may get you 'knocked into a cocked hat'?

... why we train Olympic athletes to be spies?

... why we call football 'soccer'?

... how you can play cards with Alexander the Great and Julius Caesar?

... why 'passing the buck' is not a 'good idea'?

ISBN 0-9551525-6-9
ISBN 978-0-9551525-6-6

DID NELSON TURN A BLIND EYE?

NELSON AND THE ROYAL NAVY

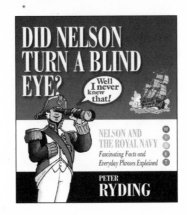

Do you know ...

... why letting 'the cat out of the bag' may leave you a 'marked man'?

... why the 'Jack and Jill' nursery rhyme is really about sex?

... why you must 'pull your finger out' before 'firing a broadside' at someone?

... why it doesn't hurt the 'monkey' when its balls are frozen off?

... the connection between shopping malls and the Battle of Trafalgar?

ISBN 0-9551525-2-6
ISBN 978-0-9551525-2-8

WHAT EVER HAPPENED TO OUR 27ᵀᴴ LETTER?

KNOWLEDGE, AND HOW WE USE IT!

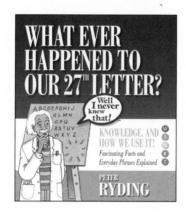

Do you know ...

... which flag gave bakers 13 to a dozen?

... why we all end sentences in Latin without even knowing it?

... what is the 27th letter of our alphabet?

... which idiot created fool's-cap paper and when did it become 'stationery'?

... how come the Sumerians gave us nothing but changed the world for ever?

ISBN 0-9551525-7-7
ISBN 978-0-9551525-7-3

Future WINKT books for release in 2007 and 2008

Log on to www.winkt.com to find out more.
Join the club and receive advance information of new releases!

- Time, Astronomy and Astrology
- Food and Drink
- London and Londoners
- Knights and Warfare through the Ages
- Big Business and Great Brands

- Ancient Greece
- USA and the World
- Cockney Rhyming Slang
- and more!

You've read the book – now play the game!

WELL I NEVER KNEW THAT – THE ADVENTURE!

The fun and fast-moving interactive **DVD** and **TV GAME** with fascinating and intriguing pictures, photos and video clues.

10 games on a DVD disc – guaranteed no repeat questions.

The perfect gift for lovers of words, phrases, history and our national heritage.

Available from www.winkt.com Autumn 2006.

Also by the same author

'Houston – we MAY have a problem!'

How to spot business issues early and fix them.

ISBN 0-9551525-9-3
ISBN 978-0-9551525-9-7

Copies can be ordered from www.peterryding.com

'I commend this book to anyone who feels they MAY be facing business challenges ... amusing and entertaining but without pulling any punches.'

SIR JOHN HARVEY-JONES MBE (of TV *Troubleshooter* fame)

'This short book is the most straightforward and digestible piece of commercial education that I have come across.'

CHIEF EXECUTIVE OF THE SOCIETY OF TURNAROUND PROFESSIONALS

In the fast-paced business world of today everyone is under more stress than ever before. That includes CEOs and their directors. No wonder they need help. But how and when should they get that help?

This book provides the answer in a very short, illustrated and highly readable way. It is written by one of the UK's leading profit improvement experts and is specifically for CEOs and their leadership teams.

It tells the story of John, a CEO with a problem.

The trouble is, it has crept up on him and he doesn't know what to do.

'King Harold is too busy to see any salesmen right now.'

In fact, he doesn't really understand the severe implications for his business and for himself personally.

He then does the first of three critical things.

He gets help.

But is it too late?

If you haven't been there before, it is very tough to spot the problem, to identify which levers to pull, to know whom to believe and how to manage the various stakeholders around you. This book shows you what to do and what not to do.

'Reading this book could be the best spent thirty minutes of your career and save you a lot more than your job!'

SIR DIGBY JONES, DIRECTOR GENERAL OF THE CBI

To contact Peter please email peter@pathfinderpro.co.uk

Surname History and Coat of Arms

Do you know the origin of your surname?
Do you know the history of your family name from the middle ages?
Do you know the coat of arms or motto associated with it?
We do!

We specialize in providing professionally researched backgrounds to surnames and first names including coat of arms where relevant.

We can provide beautiful manuscript-style scrolls either framed or unframed.

We can provide two coats of arms side by side for a special wedding or anniversary present.

We can even provide the history of a friend's or relative's first name and surname for a very personal and treasured historical gift.

Log on to www.WINKT.com and order yours now!